INFORMATION
AND SOCIETY

The MIT Press Essential Knowledge Series

INFORMATION
AND SOCIETY

MICHAEL BUCKLAND

The MIT Press | Cambridge, Massachusetts | London, England

This book was set in Chaparral Pro by Toppan Best-set Premedia Limited. Printed and bound in the United States of America.

Library of Congress Cataloging-in-Publication Data is available.

ISBN: 978-0-262-53338-6

10   9   8   7   6   5   4   3   2   1

CONTENTS

SERIES FOREWORD

The MIT Press Essential Knowledge series offers accessible, concise, beautifully produced pocket-size books on topics of current interest. Written by leading thinkers, the books in this series deliver expert overviews of subjects that range from the cultural and the historical to the scientific and the technical.

In today's era of instant information gratification, we have ready access to opinions, rationalizations, and superficial descriptions. Much harder to come by is the foundational knowledge that informs a principled understanding of the world. Essential Knowledge books fill that need. Synthesizing specialized subject matter for nonspecialists and engaging critical topics through fundamentals, each of these compact volumes offers readers a point of access to complex ideas.

Bruce Tidor
Professor of Biological Engineering and Computer Science
Massachusetts Institute of Technology

It is a truism to say that we live in an "information age" or an "information society," but it is nonetheless impossible to deny that information (along with data and knowledge, if we wish to make to make the distinction) is now central to the functioning of all developed societies.

It is conventional to suggest that we came to this situation through a series of "information revolutions," by which a new technology, using the word in its broadest sense, drastically changed the way information is recorded and communicated. The number and nature of these revolutions varies between commentators, but typically they include the introduction of writing, printing, mass communications, the digital computer, and the Internet.

A cogent analysis by Luciano Floridi argues that we are living in an age of "hyperhistory," in which the well-being of individuals and societies is entirely dependent on information and communication technologies. Floridi's contention is that we are seeing an "informational turn" or "fourth revolution," following the scientific revolutions of Copernicus, Darwin and Freud (Floridi 2014). We should regard ourselves as informationally embodied organisms, "inforgs," embedded in an informational environment, the "infosphere," in which the boundaries between our online and offline environments merge.

Given this embedded centrality of information in modern society, it is not surprising that it is studied, from various points of view, by a number of disciplines, including computer science, media studies, psychology, sociology, mathematics, education, economics, and philosophy. These are only the disciplines interested in information in the sense of meaningful, communicable information. The list lengthens if we include conceptions of information in other domains, such as physics and biology (Robinson and Bawden 2013).

The one discipline that has information as its sole object of interest is information science. This grew during the twentieth century from the concerns of the "documentation movement," which sought to understand the nature of documents of all kinds, and hence to provide access to them in a much more sophisticated way than conventional catalogs and indexes could provide (Wright 2014). The advent of the digital computer gave an impetus to the new discipline, which has overlapped with, while remaining distinct from, computer science. Information science concerns itself with all aspects of the organization and communication of recorded information, with the information and digital literacies needed to make use of it, and with associated ethical issues. The insights of the discipline are crucially relevant in developing the dramatically changing infosphere.

There are a number of good texts setting out the basics of information science; I am co-author of one such (Bawden and Robinson 2012). But these are typically aimed internally: at faculty, students, and practitioners within the subject. If we believe, as I do, that information science has many insights to offer to a much wider context, then we need books that specifically address a wider audience. Michael Buckland's book is the first to attempt this.

An impressive feature of the book is the way in which such a breadth of material is brought together clearly and concisely. It is pleasing to see how Buckland integrates the "traditional concerns" of information science—in particular, how information resources are described, organized and retrieved, and the ways in which people and groups behave with information—with thoughts about the nature of the documents through which recorded information is communicated. The new forms of document which have emerged in networked digital environments have led to a renewed interest in the nature of documents, and this kind of conceptual analysis, though lower key than new technological developments, is just as likely to be valuable in ensuring effective communication, and good use, of information. I applaud Buckland's vision of information science as a broad and inclusive field of study; only such a holistic approach can do justice to the issues that emerge when information takes center stage in society.

Michael Buckland modestly writes that his interpretation draws on the work of many people and little of it is original. While this may be true in the sense that the material presented in his book has mostly been published before in some form, I think there is great originality in the way it has been selected, organized and presented for a nonspecialist audience. This is highly commendable, and the book deserves to be widely read. Its success will, perhaps, be measured by whether it is the first of a succession of publications, bringing the insights of information science and the documentation movements to a wider audience. We must hope that proves to be the case, as these perspectives are sorely needed if the infosphere is to develop and flourish.

David Bawden
Centre for Information Science, City University London

References

Bawden, David, and Lyn Robinson. 2012. *Introduction to information science*. London: Facet.

Floridi, Luciano. 2014. *The fourth revolution: How the infosphere is reshaping human reality*. Oxford: Oxford University Press.

Robinson, Lyn, and David Bawden. 2013. Mind the gap: Transitions between concepts of information in varied domains. In *Theories of information, communication and knowledge: A multidisciplinary approach*, ed. Fidelia Ibekwe-SanJuan and Thomas Dousa, 121–141. Berlin: Springer.

Wright, Alex. 2014. *Cataloging the world: Paul Otlet and the birth of the information age*. New York: Oxford University Press.

PREFACE

We now live, we are told, in an *information society* and this is considered to be a very important development. But what does it mean? And what are the consequences? In answer, we offer a short informal introduction to ways in which *information* and *society* are related and to our ever-increasing dependence on a vast increase in documents and data of many kinds.

The word *information* is used here in an ordinary, everyday way. Other, specialized uses in law, statistics, thermodynamics, cryptography, and elsewhere we leave to others. We are concerned with information as influencing what we know, with the role of communication and, especially, recorded information, in our daily lives, and with how information is found. We are, therefore, concerned with beliefs, social agendas, and changing technologies. These are complex areas that resist simple, formal explanation. There are conceptual and theoretical difficulties that we will mention but do not claim to solve. Our purpose is to provide a descriptive introduction which draws on the work of many people and little of it is original. Since it is an elementary introduction, the detailed citing of sources ordinarily found in academic writing is not provided. However, much of the text is adapted from earlier publications which are identified in the Further Reading section at the end where some additional sources are also suggested.

I thank Wayne de Fremery for his insight on Information Theory, Wayne Heiser for help with Zublin's letter, and Lisa Börjesson, Colin B. Burke, Vivien Petras, and Lin "David" Wang for their helpful comments on early versions of the text.

INTRODUCTION

The word *information* has been used with several different meanings. In this book we are concerned with information in society, in everyday human experience. So we may call this *realistic* information science and distinguish it from studies associated with statistical and other technical analyses in cryptanalysis, signaling systems, thermodynamics, and other areas (*formal* information science). Specialized, technical uses of the word *information* unrelated to human knowing and everyday experience are outside our scope. Our scope can be illustrated by considering a passport, a rather complex document that plays a powerful role in social control.

We are concerned with human perception, social behavior, changing technologies, and issues of trust. So what we examine will often be complex, untidy, or unclear, and this prevents simple, satisfactory scientific analyses.

The growing importance of information derives from the progressive division of labor, which characterizes our transition from hunters and gatherers to an increasingly complex society. We depend more and more on others, which requires coordination and communication and means, in practice, dependence on information. This is not a simple or neutral situation, because many others seek to advance their agendas by using different forms of information to shape our beliefs and behaviors in ways they want.

Information

Use of the word *information* increased greatly during the twentieth century and has developed many different meanings. The lack of settled terminology and figurative use, as in *information society*, make discussion difficult. The lack of agreement on its meaning makes it suitable for slogans and for enthusiastic metaphors. Anyone wishing to be precise and clear should either declare the particular meaning being used or, better, use some other, more precise word or phrase (such as *data*, *record*, *document*, or *knowledge imparted*), since for each of the principal meanings of the word *information* there is also another suitable, more specific word.

We depend more and more on others, which requires coordination and communication and means, in practice, dependence on information.

Words get used in creative ways, and there are differences in the way they are used in different contexts. Multiple words may be used to refer to an individual thing, while individual words are commonly ambiguous, used to refer to multiple different things. English words ending in "-ation" are usually ambiguous, referring variously to a process, an event, an object, or an outcome. (Consider *communication* and *regulation*.) The character string "i n f o r m a t i o n" has been used to refer to many different things. So any simple assertion in the form "Information is ..." has little meaning and encourages confusion unless it is made clear which of the meanings is intended.

In the middle of the twentieth century, the word *information* was adopted as a technical term (notably as *information theory*) in engineers' calculations of reliability in telephony and similar signaling systems. This use related the word *information* to a series of developments in logic, probability, and computation that proved very fertile in some important fields, notably cryptanalysis, electrical engineering, and thermodynamics. In these developments, it is ordinarily assumed that information is true, knowledge is true, and differences can be rendered as bits. But these important technical developments and assumptions about the truth value of information have little overlap with everyday human experience, so it is important to recognize that there are *two* fields of study, both of which have used the name *information science*, but they have little in common beyond using the same name. Each seems to have limited interest in, or relevance to, the other.

We can make an analogy with philology, the field in the humanities concerned with the examination of texts. Here a distinction is made between examination of the text itself, known as *the lower criticism*, and the examination of a text in its material and sociohistorical context, *the higher criticism*. We might, comparably, refer to the *lower information science* and the *higher information science*, or, more diplomatically, make a distinction between *formal* and *realistic* approaches to the study of information.

In this book, we are concerned with information in relation to everyday human experience, and thus with the complex multiplicity of messages, records, documents, and perceptions in our lives; the difficulties associated with meaning and finding the most relevant information; and the need to trust sources and documents. This, then, is an introduction to "higher," or *realistic*, information science in its cultural context rather than the *formal* information science described above and discussed elsewhere.

We need to include more than the study of what are traditionally called documents, because we communicate through gesture, language, and the use of material objects. Our central theme is that in modern society, interpersonal relationships are increasingly *indirect*, through messages, records, and other forms of document. In what follows, *information* is used in an ordinary, everyday sense with two related meanings: (1) what we infer from gestures, language, texts, and other objects; and (2) material forms of communication—bits, books, and other kinds of physical messages and records. We start with an example.

My Passport

My passport is more powerful than I am, because I cannot cross frontiers without it, but it could cross them without me. This small, printed booklet seems, at first sight, to be a good example of the static nature of traditional media. But the inside is more complex. It has multiple and often changing components. There is a photograph of me and my handwritten signature. There are marks for optical character recognition inside the front cover and a bar code inside the back cover, each of which make it a digital document capable of being read into computers. The pages became filled up with marks stamped by frontier officials that record my travels, and extra pages were added to accommodate more. Additional documents have been inserted: elaborate visas issued by the Chinese, Russian, and Vietnamese governments that provided income for them and permission for me. A biometric security code was inserted at Heathrow Airport, and some small security stickers have been attached to the back cover. A more recently issued passport would also include a chip capable of transmitting my name, nationality, gender, birthday, birthplace, and portrait.

My passport is going to expire, as I will also. The passport's expiration date, unlike mine, is exactly known and, unlike mine, easily extended with a small fee for renewal. So although parts of my passport are carefully designed to prevent alteration, it is physically dynamic, as are many other types of information, especially those in electronic form. Even the most conventional document, writing on paper, is technology. Technology is now increasingly electronic—so-called information technology—as if pen and paper were not information technologies.

The social aspect of my passport is clear when we remember that it is not really the passport itself that allows me to cross frontiers or board airplanes, but guards enforcing regulations. In remote areas where there is no physical barrier, I could cross a frontier with or without a passport; illegally, perhaps, but it could be done. If the frontier is not well marked, I might even cross it unintentionally. So the power of my passport does not arise simply from the document itself, but from more or less enforced social regulations within which passports are used as an evidentiary device within a system of controls embedded in complex bureaucratic systems.

Strictly speaking, a government can only control (or try to control) its own borders, not those of other countries, but acceptance of the validity of my passport extends internationally through requests and agreements. I used to carry a British passport that had an impressive printed page elegantly inscribed with a statement reminiscent of a nineteenth-century imperialist power: "Her Britannic Majesty's Secretary of State requests and requires in the name of Her Majesty all those whom it may concern to allow the bearer to pass freely without let or hindrance and to afford the bearer such assistance and protection as may be necessary."

There is a cognitive aspect as well. A guard needs to examine the passport in order to be satisfied that the document is in order; that—judging from the description and portrait in it—it is, in fact, *my* passport and not somebody else's, and that it has not expired. If a fake passport appeared to be in order and seemed to belong to the bearer, then it would be accepted and the traveler would be allowed to pass. Passports work on trust, not on truth.

Because a false or altered passport would be trusted if it appeared correct, forged and stolen passports have value for individuals not eligible for a valid passport of the kind they would like or who prefer for some reason to travel using a false identity. In 1994, my passport was stolen when abroad, and the local US embassy issued me a replacement passport clearly marked as valid for one year only. It was later renewed for another nine years, but the renewal statement was hidden inside the back. So for nine years this renewed passport appeared at first sight to have expired. Most guards noticed the original expiration date and then looked for evidence of renewal, but a significant number did not notice the expiration because they expected travelers to have current passports and did not examine it carefully enough to see that mine had apparently expired.

Frontier guards now usually run the passport's machine-readable code through a reader, and so delegate verification to some remote machine that compares the passport's codes with records already stored there. In other words, the guardian role is partly delegated to machine-readable codes, reading devices, and, somewhere, a machine programmed to respond to the encoded evidence. The human guard only needs to see that I resemble sufficiently the photographic portrait in the passport. Biometric technology has been developed to which that visual task could be delegated, so it is not hard to imagine a passport control station operating without any direct action by a human guard, much as grocery stores and libraries have experimented with self-service checkout.

The passport is evidence offered as a substitute for firsthand knowledge of a person's identity and citizenship. Its use depends on social regulations backed by military force, and also on cognitive activity: the guard has to read it and believe that the passport is valid and that it is being used by the proper bearer. Finally, the machine-readable codes make it into a piece of machinery engaged in complex systems.

This small, printed booklet is a complex, dynamic, multimedia device with print, manuscript, and machine-readable scripts. It is carefully designed both to resist improper alteration and also to be changed in permitted ways. The passport plays a significant social role as a device used to control personal travel, and it is also widely used to serve other purposes when establishing one's identity is needed, for example, when boarding an airplane or dealing with a bank. This combination of varied physical features, cognitive perceptions of it as trustworthy, and use as a tool for social control makes it a rich example. Modern passports came into use a century ago, and the role, complexity, and powerful affordances of my passport make it a suitable emblem of contemporary society.

The Division of Labor and the Need to Know

The shift to dependence on documents has a long history. Cultures have developed from hunting and gathering to agriculture, industry, and sophisticated services. Common themes in these developments are the division of labor and increased interdependence of people and institutions.

As individuals, very few of us grow our own crops, kill the animals we eat, milk cows ourselves, or grow our own coffee beans. Similarly, we do not, by ourselves, make the technology we use, construct the buildings we live in, or generate the energy resources we depend on. Instead, we depend on others.

The division of labor allows us a higher standard of living through the development of specialized skills and greater efficiency from economies of scale, but, in consequence, we have become much more dependent on each other in many ways. We rely increasingly on other people, on technology, and on the infrastructure of transportation, financial services, regulations, and other developments that make this interdependence possible. Others, in turn, depend on us.

The exchange of goods and services requires markets, and markets depend on knowing what choices are available and on what terms. Markets are information systems. The better-informed buyers and sellers are, the more perfect the market is said to be. Less often stated is that markets and this interdependence also require an increase in communication and documentation. If we are to buy goods and services instead of providing our own, then we need to know who provides what we want, how much we shall need to pay, and whether what is offered is what we think it is. We can ask, of course, but mostly we depend (and anybody we ask will depend) on documents: price lists, content descriptions, warranties, availability, limitations, and so on. Since we cannot ascertain entirely by ourselves everything we would like to know, we have no choice but to depend on what others tell us, and so we must also decide whom and what to trust. In this situation, it is unrealistic to make a distinction between believing and knowing. What you know is what you believe. The more confident you are in a belief, the more likely you are to consider it knowledge.

The increasing dependence on the knowledge of others—on "secondhand knowledge"—has two aspects: the ever-increasing division of labor, which makes us more dependent on others; and the ever-increasing reliance on communication (mostly documents) for the coordination that interdependence requires.

Culture and society develop through communication and collaboration. But, increasingly, we cannot communicate directly person to person. The best we can do is to use documents that record what that other person said, wrote, or did. The work of others and their ideas are incorporated in documents, both by them and about them, much as technology incorporates the labor of past inventors. Viewed this way, documents have become the connecting tissue that enables complex societies to function. Documents have increasingly become the means for monitoring, influencing, and negotiating relationships with others.

Documents have increasingly become the means for monitoring, influencing, and negotiating relationships with others.

Agendas of Others

The differing forms of documents and varied motivations
in their use are reflected in the case of a letter written
in May 1856 by Llewellyn Zublin to his son in Iowa about
the dramatic murder of a newspaperman on a San Fran-
cisco street. The letter was later acquired by a dealer, who
sold it to Berkeley's Bancroft Library for its collections
supporting research on the history of California. In 2000,
the letter was photocopied, keyed into a computer, and a
printout produced, which was then used as copy by students in a class on hand-press printing. The students re-
produced the letter as a pamphlet. Some extra copies of
this elegant booklet were retained by the Bancroft library
for possible use in its fund-raising. In 2001, one of the
student printers reconstructed the history of this text
in its successive formats for an assignment in a seminar
on document theory—and, now, we use it as an example
that shows the distinction between a text and text-bearing
documents and involves quite varied forms of document
(handwritten letter, photocopy, digital file, computer
printout, and hand-press printing). It also reflects very
varied motivations: family friendship, commerce, support
for historical research, technical training, a library's
fund-raising, obtaining educational credit, and academic
theorizing.

It is not only our own needs that should concern us in understanding the role of information in society, but also the agendas of others. Examples are easy to find:

- schools use textbooks to guide our learning and to control teachers.

- religions use sacred texts to inspire particular beliefs and obedience.

- artists produce images to please and challenge us.

- merchants invest heavily in advertisements to influence what we buy.

- politicians make statements to seek votes and support for their campaigns.

- entertainers use varied media to amuse us and generate income from us.

- individuals use messages to communicate and attract attention.

- museums use the selective presentation and interpretation of objects to explain the past.

- mass media constantly transmit programs to entertain us, influence us, and satisfy advertisers.

- libraries provide access to selective collections of documents to facilitate our reading.

• social media allow the very rapid dissemination of comments.

• recording devices are used to monitor our purchases, movements, and behavior.

This list could be extended indefinitely. As the list builds up, we see more and more of our lives included. The choice of examples is less important than the cumulative evidence that our lives are permeated by messages, records, and documents used to influence our behavior and to shape our culture.

Information Society

Any claim that our "information society" is special or remarkable implies a contrast with some other "non-information society" that is different in some noteworthy way. But since all groups, and by extension all societies, develop their collective character through shared activity, through collaboration and communication, a "non-information society" would be a contradiction in terms.

It is unlikely that medieval people were less talkative than modern people. The significant difference between the most-developed current societies and less-developed societies cannot be the fact that information itself is more important but, rather, that some aspects of development referred to by the phrase *information society* involve wider use of information. My passport and the examples on the list provide an explanation. The passport is a nonoral form of information: a document. We can see that although the actions themselves are mostly not, in themselves, new, changes in technology have facilitated a greatly increased activity. The real change is in the rise of records. It would be more accurate to speak of an emerging *document society*.

Truth, Trust, and Belief

A traditional, academic view is that knowledge is *justified true belief*, that information, which leads to knowledge, must therefore be true, by definition, and that knowledge is (or could be) composed of a series of propositions. But even in the world of analytical philosophy, this is problematic, except for the understanding that knowledge is belief. In our daily lives, the presumption that all information is, by definition, true has no basis in common sense or personal experience. We may want to know if a statement is true, and we may well be doubtful, but in practice we usually end up trusting the evidence, an expert, a wise person, or a friend. Without trust, we would be paralyzed. Our relationship with documents is based on trust, which becomes more necessary as well as more problematic as communications become less and less direct.

Referring to the patterns in the physical universe as "information" appears redundant or metaphorical. The characteristics of the universe (shapes, forms, patterns, physical processes, and so on) are what they are, and so issues of truth do not arise. Calling all physical differences *information* seems more confusing than helpful.

The Structure of This Book

We started by emphasizing our concern with information in everyday life, with a realistic approach to documents and data, rather than with more formalistic analyses in engineering. After some cautionary comments on uses of the word *information*, we then considered how a passport and a handwritten letter reveal the pervasive roles of documents in society, both in enabling the division of labor and in the advancement of many different agendas.

The following chapters note the rising flood of data, documents, and records of many kinds and the way they are used as well as analyses of how we cope with information. Chapter 2, "Document and Evidence," reviews different meanings of the word information, outlines the dramatic long-term growth of documents and data (the "information explosion"), and notes the rise of techniques and initiatives to handle their organization, discovery, and use. Chapter 3, "Individual and Community," examines what individuals do with information, what communities know, the central role of culture, and how there are always physical, mental, and social aspects to information. Chapter 4, "Organizing: Arrangement and Description," is a summary of how collected documents are arranged and described so that we can identify and find a copy when needed. Chapter 5, "Naming," considers the nature and complexity of describing. Chapter 6, "Metadata," discusses how document descriptions, also known as metadata, are used for two purposes: to characterize documents and, by making indexes, to find the ones we want. Chapter 7, "Discovery and Selection," introduces the matching of queries and metadata for locating known documents and the more difficult task of identifying previously unknown documents likely to be of interest. Chapter 8, "Evaluation of Selection Methods," explains the standard evaluation of selection methods and acknowledges problems with relevance. The final chapter, "Summary and Reflections," repeats key points from earlier chapters and considers some of their implications for how we should understand information in society.

DOCUMENT AND EVIDENCE

The word *information* commonly refers to bits, bytes, books, and other signifying objects, and it is convenient to refer to this class of objects as *documents,* using a broad sense of that word. Documents are important because they are considered as evidence, and so there are cognitive and cultural as well as physical aspects to them. Writing, printing, telecommunications, and copying allow documents to be made more available across space and time, and there has been an enormous increase in documents of many kinds, most recently in the form of vast digital data sets ("big data") for which we are not well prepared. Techniques are needed to organize this rising mass of material so that one can discover the most suitable resources for any given purpose. There are several quite diverse requirements for later use of documents and, as in any developing field, terminology has been inconsistent and often quite figurative.

Information as Thing

We have noted that during the twentieth century the word *information* became fashionable and was used in many ways. Some writers extended *information* to denote patterns unrelated to human knowing. Others have limited the meaning to true statements or to the reduction of uncertainty. Most of the meanings that have to do with human knowing fall into one of three categories:

1.   information as *knowledge*, meaning the knowledge imparted;

2.   information as *process*, the process of becoming informed; and

3.   information as *thing*, denoting bits, bytes, books, and other physical media. In effect, this, the commonest use of the word, includes any material thing or physical action perceived as signifying. In this third sense, *information* becomes a synonym for a broad view of *document*.

Document, as a verb, means to make evident, to provide an explanation. *Document*, as a noun, was historically something you learned from, including a lesson, a lecture, or an example. Gradually, document came increasingly to mean a written text, while retaining a sense of evidence. Nevertheless, the definition of *document* has remained unsettled, and three views of it can be identified:

1. a conventional, material view. The everyday, conventional view of documents is of graphic records, usually text, written on a flat surface (paper, clay tablet, microfilm, word processor files, etc.) that are material, local, and, generally, transportable. These objects are made as documents. The limits of inclusion are unclear.

2. an instrumental view. Almost anything can be made to serve as a document, to signify something, to be held up as constituting evidence of some sort. Natural history collections and archeological traces can be included in this view. Before the adoption of military uniforms, it was hard for a soldier in battle to know who was a friend and who was an enemy. In a sixth-century battle between Welsh and Saxons, fought in a field of leeks, Saint David instructed the Welsh to indicate their identity to each other by wearing a leek. The leek documented Welsh identity to those who understood the code and remains today a national symbol of Wales. In her manifesto *What Is Documentation*? Suzanne Briet's discussion of documents examined documents made of or from objects. She

famously asserted that a newly discovered species of antelope, when positioned in a taxonomy and placed in a cage, was made to serve as a document. This view follows from her assertion that bibliography is properly considered to be concerned with access to evidence, not just to texts.

3. a semiotic view. The two previous views emphasize the creation of documents and imply intentional creation. So they are incomplete from a semiotic view, in which anything could be considered a document if it is regarded as evidence of something, regardless of what the creator (if any) of that object intended (if anything).

The importance of a document depends on how we understand it, since the ability to make sense and respond is what enables living organisms to survive. Documents and documentation constitute evidence that may be useful to us in making sense of our situation and options. Documents are used as intermediaries between ourselves and others, and we judge documents in varied ways. We try to understand what we see. We decide how far we trust what we perceive, and how we feel about what we see influences us. How accessible it appears to be and how easy to use both strongly influence whether we bother with it. We "make do" (satisfice) rather than optimize.

We also need to distinguish between meaning and sense. A sentence can be meaningful, yet not make sense.

"A mouse swallowed the elephant" is a grammatically meaningful statement, but it does not make sense in any realistic context, although it could in cartoons or other imaginary contexts. We commonly construct sense when there is uncertain or incomplete meaning, such as abstract art or Rorschach images.

Documents and Document Anatomy

Documentation—the management of documents—leads to the question: with what kinds of document is documentation concerned? Clearly, digital and printed texts have been the primary concern, but once one accepts the notion of documents as objects from which one may learn, handwritten manuscripts should also be included, and there is no basis for limiting the scope to texts. Since diagrams, drawings, maps, and photographs are used to describe or explain, images should not be excluded. If printed maps are included, then there is no rational basis for excluding terrestrial globes, which are three-dimensional maps. And, if diagrams are included, why not also three-dimensional models and educational toys? If three-dimensional objects are included, museum specimens and expressive sculpture cannot reasonably be excluded. If written language is included, then why not recorded, spoken language or music? And if recorded speech and music are included, why not recorded performances? And if recorded performances, why not live performances?

Anything regarded as a document can be seen as having the following four aspects.

1.   Significance. There is a phenomenological aspect to documents. So long as documents are objects perceived as signifying something, the status of being a document is not inherent (essential), but attributed to an object. Meaning is always constructed by a viewer.

2.   Cultural codes. All forms of communicative expression depend on some shared understanding, which can be thought of as language in a broad sense.

3.   Media type. Different types of expression have evolved: texts, images, numbers, diagrams, art, music, dance, and so on.

4.   Physical medium. Media include clay tablets, paper, film, magnetic tape, punch cards, and so on, sometimes in combination, as in a passport.

The status of being a document, therefore, is attributive (1), and every document has cultural (2), type (3), and physical (4) aspects. Genres are culturally and historically situated combinations. Being digital directly affects only the physical medium, but, like the invention of paper and of printing, the consequences are extensive.

It is reasonable to refer to any object that has documentary characteristics as a document, but, of course, that does not mean it should be considered only as a document. Leeks are not always and only symbols of Welshness. The same is true in reverse, even for an archetypal document: a printed book can make a convenient doorstop, a role that depends on its physicality, not on any documentary aspect.

The History of Information Technology

The use of gesture and speech is transitory and highly localized. To see or hear you must be present there and then, but technologies have steadily reduced these limitations.

Writing

By recording, writing provides an alternative to speech. Writing can put speech, which is local and ephemeral, into a new and enduring form. Since the statement or image remains, it can be seen at a future time, and, being portable, it can overcome effects of distance as well as time. And writing is not limited to the recording of speech and gesture. It can simply be an original inscription, commonly a record that something has happened (history) or that something should be done (agenda).

In all cases, the effect is to establish a trace, evidence that can be perceived by others or serve as a reminder for oneself. In this way, the written record can endure and overcome the passage of time for as long as the record remains legible.

A single record can, in principle, be read by anyone anywhere. Although it can be in only one place at any given point in time, the effect is to provide continuity. Writing, then, diminishes the effect of time and so provides a partial alternative to human memory, an artificial "external memory." Much has been written on the consequences of the invention of writing in providing an enduring form of evidence, thereby facilitating communication, control, and commerce. It is very hard now to imagine life without writing.

Writing in the sand is washed away. Ink fades. Paper can burn or disintegrate. Electronic records are very fragile. But, within its limits, writing exceeds speech or gesture with the advantage of being able to counteract the effects of time and, by also being portable, of distance.

Printing
Printing provides multiplication of writing, and so extends the effect of writing with two consequences. First, while a piece of writing can conquer distance by being moved, it can still only ever be in one place at one time. Printing makes copies that can be in as many different

Within its limits, writing exceeds speech or gesture with the advantage of being able to counteract the effects of time and, by also being portable, of distance.

places as copies have been made. The more widely copies are scattered, the more convenient for geographically dispersed individuals. This matters, because convenience of access is a powerful determinant of use.

Second, since any individual record is vulnerable to alteration, including falsification and destruction, there is safety in numbers. The more copies that are made and the more widely they are distributed, the more difficult it becomes to alter them and the more likely that one or more copies will survive.

Making communication permanent in a record that is an alternative to human memory and distributing many copies has far-reaching consequences. The use of print facilitated the Renaissance, the development of science, and the rise of the modern state. Much has been written on the impact of printing.

Telecommunication

Until well into the nineteenth century, telecommunication was a person on foot, horse, or ship bringing good news or bad. The rise of transmission technologies, notably railways, telegraph, telephone, radio, and now the Internet, have had the effect of reducing the effects of distance and diminishing the delays associated with travel. Telecommunications, like printing, facilitated managerial coordination and commercial propaganda and here, too, there is a large literature.

Copying

Transcribing texts is as old as writing. In the eighteenth century, handwritten documents were copied by "letter press." A thin moist sheet of paper was pressed against the original so that some of the ink of the original would transfer into the moist sheet. Documents were occasionally photographed during the nineteenth century, but generating rapid, reliable, economical copies of documents is a twentieth-century development, with three important techniques: photostat, microfilm, and electrostatic copying (xerography, dry writing). (The numerous forms of duplicating that involve the creation of a new original are more properly regarded as small-run printing). There has been much less historical and social commentary on the impact of copying technology.

Photostat—direct-projection photography onto sensitized paper without an intermediate negative—was pioneered by René Graffin of the Institut Catholique in Paris to facilitate his editing of early Christian writings in Syriac. The image produced was negative (white writing in a black ground). The left-to-right reversal was corrected by using a 45-degree mirror. His equipment received a prize in the International Exposition in Paris in 1900, and a few photostat cameras were built for European libraries, but there was little impact until photostat equipment became commercially available in 1910. The speed, accuracy, and efficiency of photostats for both text and images compared with manual transcription or typewritten copies were quickly recognized. The photostat process was widely adopted and became the copying process of choice at least until the late 1930s.

Microfilm carried by carrier pigeons was famously used by René Dagron to transport messages across enemy lines during the siege of Paris in 1870–71, but widespread use came only in the 1930s, when compact precision cameras, standard film speeds, and 35 mm safety film became available. Banks, newspapers, libraries, and other organizations adopted microfilm and its variants on a large scale.

Electrostatic copying, better known as xerography ("dry writing"), was developed to replace photostats, became widely used during the 1960s, and is today the technology of choice for copying and for printing digital documents.

Making legible copies from varied originals is not, in practice, separable from image enhancement. A faded document may need contrast enhancement to be made more legible. Using ultraviolet light can reveal erased text on a reused medieval manuscript, and infrared light may reveal text that a censor has inked over. Thus, copying involves more than merely making copies. We see by means of light radiated or reflected from some surface, so a legible image is one where the contrast in light is suitable for human vision. It is not surprising, then, that the photographic copying of documents quickly expanded to the use of techniques (different light sources, filters, fluorescence, and special emulsions) to render legible copies of humanly illegible originals.

The primary effect of these technologies is to reduce the effects of both time and space. Records became increasingly accessible in any place and at any time, making it easy to read what would otherwise have been forgotten. These technologies amplify the effects of each other and can be combined. A good example is the use of photography to make an image of something on a printing plate (photolithography) to print many copies of it.

These developments were greatly enhanced by successive advances in engineering, such as the use of steam engines, electricity, photography and, especially now, digital computing and communication. These technologies have enabled massive increases in the number of documents. In the nineteenth century, people worried about the "information flood." In the twentieth century, it became the "information explosion"—and now, everything that came before is dwarfed by "big data."

The Rise of Data Sets

Academic research projects typically generate data sets, but in practice it is generally impractical for anyone else to attempt to make further use of these data, even though

In the nineteenth century, people worried about the "information flood." In the twentieth century, it became the "information explosion"—and now, everything that came before is dwarfed by "big data."

major funders of research now mandate that researchers have a data management plan to preserve generated data sets and make them accessible.

Science and engineering are constructive enterprises evolving through hypotheses and model building, trial and error, and testing and revision. For this reason, shared access to the record of prior work is critical. Historically, the record has been primarily textual, in the form of published technical reports, articles, conference papers, books, and other genres, although there were always some nontextual records, such as images, numerical tables, and collected specimens.

Print-on-paper materials are made accessible through a slowly evolved infrastructure of scholarly norms (including acknowledgment and citation), genres of technical writing, specialized publishers and distribution channels, libraries and bibliographies, catalogs and indexes. The infrastructure for publishing and bibliographical access was established by scholars, societies, librarians, and publishers. During the second half of the twentieth century, digital methods made additional search techniques feasible. (One thinks of *Chemical Abstracts*, Medline, and the *Science Citation Index*.) It is a creaky system, but it works.

No comparable infrastructure is yet in place for data sets. If one were to pick a random selection of papers reporting the results of projects completed five or 10 years ago and ask to reuse the datasets they were based on, the effort would probably generate more embarrassment and frustration than success.

If these data sets are regarded as illustrative appendages to a definitive textual record, then this situation is regrettable. However, the situation is worse than that, because the practice of science and engineering has also been transformed by the pervasive adoption of digital computation. The potentially useful record of scholarship, even in the humanities, is increasingly not written reports, but (mainly nontextual) digital data sets of many kinds. The raw material, the operations upon it, and progressively more refined derivations can be beneficially shared and built upon by other researchers, not only in the same field but also in adjacent fields. This extends the impact and broadens the evidence in ways not practical using textual reports alone and has enabled a rise in computationally intensive, data-centric scholarship. The potential now exists, therefore, for a far greater return on investment in research. But there is a requirement. The infrastructure of well-developed work practices, publication norms, libraries, and bibliographical access that evolved to create and sustain an accessible archive of the literature of each field has to be complemented by a corresponding set of work practices and infrastructure for the archive of digital resources that constitute an ever-increasing proportion of the record.

Researchers tend to work within domains and in relatively narrow research fronts, with informal interpersonal interaction within each specialty. Within a specialized field, researchers commonly know each other, or, at least, of each other. They graduate from similar programs, work in teams, meet in conferences, read the same journals, and correspond by email. These informal social networks strongly complement or replace formal channels of communication and documentation. In interaction between research fronts, however, this informal social network is largely absent. Without membership in the same "invisible college," researchers are unlikely to know what they could ask for or whom they could ask, and they are less likely to receive cooperation.

Rich results can be obtained when researchers explore at or over the boundaries of their fields and encounter ideas or data that are relevant but new and different (for them). This is why research funders and academic planners have long tried to encourage interdisciplinary interactions in the strongly discipline-based academic environment. A resource that can be made to provide benefit to more than one group yields a greater return on the investment.

There are examples of good practices in the very largest of science projects and in social science numeric data series, but widespread and largely undocumented deficiencies exist elsewhere. The significance of the problem can be understood by imagining that a large proportion of the textual record was written but never published, and so remains largely unknown or inaccessible and likely to be lost. What a waste!

Some Practical Initiatives

Our memories cannot retain everything we might wish to remember. Organizations as well as individuals need records. Thus, increasing quantities of documents are retained as a kind of artificial "external memory," with two consequences: first, the explosion of documents and their complexity increase problems of knowing what to trust. Second, to cope with this explosion, a fifth vector of technical development became necessary for finding and selecting the most suitable documents as and when needed. This fifth vector has had various names, including bibliography, documentation, information retrieval, and information science.

Collections of documents (libraries) were traditionally supervised by knowledgeable scholars, whose familiarity with the collection enabled them to recommend the most suitable documents for any purpose. This approach is unreliable, however, because scholar-librarians become forgetful, move away, or die. Martin Schrettinger, a Bavarian monk turned librarian, was conscious of this problem and asserted the need for systems, instead of persons, for finding and retrieving documents. He coined the term "Library science" (*Bibliothek-Wissenschaft*) for his textbook of 1808. A political refugee from Italy, Sir Anthony Panizzi developed sound cataloging practices for the library of the British Museum. In the United States, Melvil Dewey promoted efficiency and standardized procedures. The techniques of modern librarianship were well developed by the end of the nineteenth century.

Libraries, however, ordinarily deal with only a limited range of published documents and with limited attention to the detail of their contents. In 1895, two Belgians, Paul Otlet and Henri La Fontaine, decided to provide a more complete solution. They started a complete and detailed index, the Universal Bibliographic Repertory, to everything in every medium everywhere for everyone anywhere: texts, images, maps, government records, statistical data, manuscripts, films, museum objects—everything.

Otlet rightly considered that most authors were too wordy, that published texts were duplicative and inefficient, and that the bound book ("codex") was an unsatisfactory design because pages and lines did not coincide with intellectual units. Also the printed book is static, fixed, and so cannot be corrected or updated. Otlet wanted to extract facts from printed books and to transfer them into a better, more flexible kind of "book" using new media. One vision, shared with the German chemist Wilhelm Ostwald and the English writer H.G. Wells, was an encyclopedia of concise factual statements, each updated as and when needed, and all linked in a web of subject indexing. At that time, filing cards were the most flexible and most promising storage technology. They used an elaborate artificial language, the Universal Decimal Classification, to describe each item in detail and to show how each was related by topic, date, and origin to each other item. The result was a kind of hypertextual network. Card technology becomes increasingly labor-intensive as more cards are added, however, and after decades of work and many millions of cards, their system could no longer be sustained.

Wilhelm Ostwald was inspired by Otlet to use his Nobel prize money to establish an institute in Munich named The Bridge (*Die Brücke*) to develop technology for intellectual work. Ostwald wanted to extract facts and concepts from books and periodicals in order to create efficient recall of recorded knowledge. New concepts and facts would be added and each element updated as needed. By 1912 Ostwald and his colleagues were writing lyrically about this "World Brain" (*Das Gehirn der Welt*). Novelist H. G. Wells promoted the same idea. Imagine a rigorously edited Wikipedia with concise factual records on cards. "World Memory" would have been more accurate than World Brain, but Ostwald wanted more. He hoped that, just as individual letters in Gutenberg's moveable type could be rearranged to form new words, so also, rather in the spirit of data mining, rearranging concepts might yield new knowledge.

Ostwald and Otlet represented a modernist view based on systems, logic, standards, machinery, efficiency, and progress, but the technology available to them was inadequate. It was also a utopian view based on a simplistic view of knowledge. Even scientific facts cannot be properly understood out of context, which has large consequences for anyone imagining that a technological system of total recall could be sufficient.

Problems of Later Use

The use of data sets generated by others in the past can be impeded in many different ways. The hard drive crashed and there was no backup, the person who could give permission cannot be found, and so on. As a result, there are several barriers to overcome. Here is one typology.

1. Discovery. Does a suitable data set exist?

2. Location. Where is a copy?

3. Deterioration. Is the copy too deteriorated or obsolete to be usable?

4. Permission. May it be used?

5. Interoperability. Is it standardized enough to be usable with acceptable effort?

6. Description. Is it clear enough what the data represent?

7. Trust. Are the lineage, version, and error rate understood and acceptable?

8. Use. Should I use it for my purpose?

These questions form a chain: if you learn that a data set existed, you may not be able to locate a copy; if you can locate a copy, it may not be usable; if it is usable, you may not be able to obtain permission; and so on. Any problem might prevent reuse.

In practice, the answers are unlikely to be a simple Yes or No. A positive answer is not, in itself, enough. The effort required to achieve a positive outcome may be too great. The decision is always situational. The willingness to invest effort depends on the perceived benefits of success and the known alternatives as well as the cost and the resources available. One may satisfice: a less perfect result requiring less effort will often be a reasonable course of action.

These barriers are different in kind and require different kinds of solutions: policies, work practices, infrastructure, remedial processing, and so on. For example, one repository has accepted datasets with the condition that the permission of the depositing researcher was required for third-party use, but with no contingency policy for when that researcher died or was unavailable. Some remedies are more feasible or more affordable than others.

A particular problem is that descriptive metadata sufficient for the original compiler of the data is unlikely to be sufficient for someone else who comes to use it, years later, who may not know what the original compiler took for granted and so did not provide an explanation.

The final question—should I use it for my purpose?–is different from the other seven because in this case responsibility rests with the potential user, the individual scholar him or herself. Yet the decision is influenced by the answers to the other seven questions, for each of which there are identifiable specialists and institutions capable of providing support. These are currently more clearly identifiable for the textual record than for data sets. Traditionally, bibliographies identify what resources exist, catalogs list where copies can be found, and now search engines support both tasks. Publishers provide copies in the short term; libraries provide copies in the long term; and so on. Arrangements for sustained access to data sets are, as yet, far less well developed.

Bibliography Reconsidered

In ancient Greece, a bibliographer was a "book-writer," a copyist who transcribed an existing text to make a new copy. When the word "bibliographer" came into use in Europe, it was used more or less interchangeably with "librarian" until library science developed as a distinct technical field in the nineteenth century. A century ago, more rigorous bibliographical techniques were developed. Although an interest in the intellectual and cultural "contents" of books was asserted, the emphasis was on technical analysis and description of the physical printed book itself, and the "new bibliography" came to be known as analytical or historical bibliography. Nevertheless, by the mid-twentieth century, "bibliographical access" or, simply, "bibliography" (used in a broad sense) were terms of choice in the print-on-paper world for the issues associated with the questions listed above. This is reflected in the subtitle of Patrick Wilson's classic 1968 analysis of the problems of organizing and selecting documents, *Two Kinds of Power: An Essay on Bibliographical Control*. But terminology changes and this broad sense of bibliography were largely displaced by "organization of information" and similar phrases. By default, the word "bibliography" increasingly had a narrower meaning: as the detailed examination of printed books as physical objects. An eloquent protest against this narrow view can be found in Donald McKenzie's *Bibliography and the Sociology of Texts*. McKenzie, a specialist in historical bibliography and textual criticism, argues persuasively for a broader approach in two ways. First, bibliography should extend beyond the text in the book to include its interpretation and social context. This has happened. Second, "text" should be interpreted widely to extend beyond writing in the printed books to include other media—notably films, maps, and digital data sets—in the sense of "document" discussed above. On this second goal, much more needs to be done.

Whether they're called bibliography or not, there are numerous areas needing attention in addition to the central issue of preservation of digital data.

Enriched description. How could existing data description ("metadata") for reusable data sets be improved or extended, cost-effectively, with clear separation and ancestry of both new and old and maximal interoperability using annotation techniques, standardized terminology, and other semantic web elements?

Cross-lingual interoperability. Strong cross-lingual issues arise when the metadata of two sets are in different languages, such as English and German. But also, since language evolves within fields of discourse, weak linguistic mismatches occur between specialized terminologies in different specialties within the same language. Retrieval performance is sensitive to these "dialect" differences. Computational linguistics can help.

Harmonization. Standards are limiting and constrain flexibility, but achieve long-term economies and resource sharing through interoperability. Multiple trade-offs are involved.

Coherence. As collections increase in size and when moving beyond text on paper, individual resources become less visible. There will need to be more focus, not only on descriptions, but also on issues and features common to most data sets, notably:

→where—place and spatial location, georeferencing.

→when—periods and calendar time, geotemporal encoding.

→data provenance—the need to be able to trace data back to its origin and justification.

→boundary issues through time—shifting political boundaries, unstable biological taxa, and so on.

→ontologies, taxonomies, and vocabularies—must be shared or interoperable across domains.

These issues apply to all kinds of resources.

World Brain and Other Imagery

Ostwald, Wells, and others like to refer to their grand encyclopedic design as a world brain, but this is a metaphor. It did not really resemble a brain or do what a living brain does. Referring to an encyclopedia as an "external memory" is closer, but no human remembering is involved. Records, if found and read, might serve as a partial alternative to human memory. Disk drives and other storage devices are referred to as "memory," but remembering is a creative act. We typically recall something of the context of what is remembered, and we tend to remember a little differently each time, either in the details or in our understanding of them. Humans can remember; technology can be used to record. Humans express meaning, documents mention.

When one looks, one quickly sees that discourse about information is very rich in figurative language that both helps and hinders: "external memory," "world brain," and many other examples attribute active, human-like behavior to inanimate objects or imply that information is somehow a vital, active force. Text has "content," documents "inform" us, computers "think," and "memes" are ideas that fly around infecting minds. Metaphors as figurative speech can help understanding and are commonly a step toward more adequate terminology, but forgetting that they are figurative leads easily to confusion and nonsense.

Summary

The word *information* commonly refers to physical stuff such as bits, books, and other physical media, or any physical thing perceived as signifying something: that is, documents, in a broad sense. Ordinarily, documents are graphic records, usually text, created or used to express some meaning. However, almost anything can be made to serve as a document, such a leek to express Welsh identity. On a semiotic view in which meaning is constructed in the mind of the viewer, any object might be perceived as signifying something and, in that sense, could be considered a document. So if we hold to the idea of documents being evidence, a wide variety of objects and actions could be regarded as being "documents" in this extended sense. Anything regarded as a document must be perceived as signifying something, depend on shared understandings ("cultural codes"), as well as having a physical form. Since prehistoric times, four kinds of technology have become increasingly important: writing, printing, telecommunication, and copying. The rising tide of documents has brought initiatives to organize them, the challenge of knowing which to trust, and imaginative metaphorical language to describe both problems and opportunities. Data sets are a type of document, but the infrastructure making digital data sets accessible for use over time is much less developed than for printed material. The requirements are in principle the same. Scholarly practices and the field known as bibliography need updating accordingly.

In the next chapter, we take a closer look at the use we make of documents, both as individuals and socially. Physical, mental, and social aspects are all always present in the use of information.

INDIVIDUAL AND COMMUNITY

Sensing significant developments in one's environment and seeking to influence others—*becoming informed* and *informing others*—are basic to survival. In human societies, these interactions are largely and increasingly achieved through documents. When we speak of a community knowing something, it commonly means that some of the individuals in a community know something. The ability to influence what is known within a group can have important political, economic, and practical consequences. What people know is a constituent part of their culture and knowing, believing, and understanding always occurs within a cultural context. In this way, information always has physical, mental, and social aspects that can never be fully separated.

What Individuals Do

All living creatures depend for survival on their ability to sense what is significant in their environment and to react appropriately. It may be a single-cell organism sensing and seeking moisture, a plant growing toward the light, an insect looking for food, or a mammal detecting a threatening predator. It might be a human engaged in intellectual debate. In every case, the living organism internally forms a perception. Well-being and even survival depend on accurate perception, but there is no guarantee that the organism has sensed accurately or interpreted correctly. There are, of course, many possible reactions depending on whether what is sensed is attractive (food, warmth, shelter, a potential mate) or a threat (a predator or other danger). Commonly there is an attempt to influence the perception of some other living organism through charm or deceit, but the attempt will not necessarily achieve its intended result.

These processes of sensing, perception, and reacting, and, also, seeking to influence the sensing, perception, and reacting of some other organism–*becoming informed* and *informing others*–are the basis of information in society. All communities, all societies, all collaborations arise through and depend on interaction and communication among members. This is evident among animals who interact through gestures and sounds. Prehistoric human societies used speech, dance, and gesture to communicate and drawings to record. What distinguishes humans from other animals is our greater complexity of language, images, and use of objects.

What do individuals do with documents? We use documents to communicate across space and time, and we seek documents in order to reduce our ignorance and for reassurance through verification. We document something by creating a record for our own purposes or for others, now or in the future. Our purpose may be aesthetic, when we read, view, write, draw, or perform for our own amusement, entertainment, spiritual or therapeutic purposes. We monitor our environment to sense what is happening around us and to us. We try to keep up or catch up with developments of interest to us, and we avoid or filter out what we cannot or do not want to deal with. These are individual acts, though possibly delegated to other individuals or machinery.

What Communities Know

It can be convenient and useful to speak of what a community knows. There are many examples of communities with some specialized knowledge: the staff of a manufacturing company, a class of students, the residents of a village, officials in a government department, scholars in an academic discipline, and so on. Photographers know what *f*64 signifies, Czechs know about the Battle of the White Mountain in 1620, physicians know how to diagnose illnesses, Christians know that Christ died to redeem mankind, and so on. Individuals outside each community are unlikely to have such knowledge or might believe differently.

Strictly speaking, only an individual living creature can know something, and that knowing ends with that individual's death. But since different people may have the same or very similar knowledge, perhaps learned from each other, what was known may remain known by others in the same community even as individuals die. A simple, superficial explanation is that any statement about the knowledge of a community is a generalization. It is a convenient way of describing what is known by all, by most, or, at least, by many individual members of a community. What they know may be significantly different from what all or most individuals in some other group know. This difference in knowledge is part of what makes the two groups different.

Attempts to determine what is known in a community (sometimes called domain analysis) are likely to be imprecise. It may not be clear who should be included in the community, and membership is often a matter of degree. Further, the notion of a community is deceptively simple. Social relationships include many sets of interpersonal relationships, and every individual is a member of many changing communities at any given time. Also, it may be hard to establish what an individual knows. My knowledge is partially evidenced by the records I keep. Records are shared by others within communities. Documents are useful in constituting a community and in facilitating the sharing of knowledge, but documents incompletely reflect what individuals know. The documents associated with a community may be more easily available than the individuals constituting the community, and it may well be more convenient to examine the documents instead of the people; but there is a risk in this, because it is an indirect and imperfect approach since documents are not people.

Nevertheless, what a group knows or believes can have important political, economic, and practical consequences. Understanding what is known in a community allows prediction of how the community is likely to react to new developments, its preparedness to cope with a disaster, its willingness to accept particular changes, and so on, so there are strong incentives to find out. As a result, ascertaining what is known can be very useful. Thus any ability to influence what a community knows is a significant source of power, and reflected in our list of agendas in chapter 1.

Statements in the form "the company knew ..." or "the United States knew ..." are usually figurative ways of stating that leaders of a company or of a country knew something even though the rest of that community might not. More complex explanations and an understanding of the mechanisms involved require attention to the role of culture.

Culture

The word *culture* is commonly used for "high culture," such as opera, classical music, art exhibitions, and other elegant but expensive activities of elites. In academic discussion, however, *culture* has a different and broader meaning. It refers to how we live our daily lives. The classic definition is by Sir Edward Tylor in 1871: "Culture or civilization, taken in its wide ethnographic sense, is that complex whole which includes knowledge, belief, art, morals, law, custom and any other capabilities and habits acquired by man as a member of society." Later definitions tend to be similar. Important for our purposes is that, in this broad sense, what each of us knows is a significant component of our culture, along with how we speak and how we dress. Hence differences between groups in what is known and in how individuals communicate are cultural differences.

No individual can know everyone else in the world, every place, every institution, every building, and every event. We cannot attend to every media outlet or publication. Each of us knows a lot less than is in principle knowable. Instead, we have a limited circle of friends and family. We know, more or less, the neighborhood we live in, the routes we travel, and a work or school environment. Our personal world is a small world, even though it includes participation in multiple, different, overlapping communities.

Some small worlds seem, culturally, smaller than others—for example, if we live on an isolated island, as a prison inmate, or among the elderly in a nursing home. When we learn, we generally learn from the people around us (parents, siblings, friends, teachers, and colleagues), and we learn from the signs and documents present in our environment. In brief, our knowledge, modes of communication, and ways of reasoning are culturally situated in our personal small world, and even the smallest personal world is complex. We can illustrate the consequences of this situation by considering facts, since documents are concerned with evidence, and evidence implies facts.

The visionary schemes of Paul Otlet were noted above. His ideas were summarized in two books published in the mid-1930s. At the same time, in Poland, the microbiologist Ludwik Fleck was developing his explanation, in his *Genesis and Development of a Scientific Fact* (1935/1979), of why concise factual encyclopedia entries sought by Otlet were inherently inadequate. Fleck claimed

Our knowledge, modes of communication, and ways of reasoning are culturally situated in our personal small world, and even the smallest personal world is complex.

that summarization becomes misleading when too much of the contextual explanation is left out. He argued that a text has to be understood in relation to three entities: the writer, the text, and the cultural habits and cultural context of the writer. And when a text is read, it is necessarily read with the cultural habits and cultural context of the reader. So there is, in effect, a double Fleck effect: not only the writer, the text, and the writer's cultural context, but also the reader, the text, and the reader's cultural context. Difficulties arise from differences between the two cultural contexts. We understand ancient, medieval, and renaissance authors with difficulty because the writer's knowledge and ways of thinking are more or less different from ours. And those writers would have difficulties understanding our current writings because they would not be familiar with our modern world. Context matters!

Others besides Fleck have examined how knowledge evolves within communities, a field often called social epistemology. These include Maurice Halbwachs' work on collective memory (also known as social memory), Michel Foucault's archeology of knowledge, Thomas Kuhn's notions of scientific revolutions and of paradigm shifts, as well as quantitative analyses of the surface phenomena of document-related behavior (bibliometrics).

An important area is our understanding of past events. Here it is helpful to distinguish between *the past*, *history*, and *heritage*. The *past* (what happened) has passed. It is gone and it is inaccessible. We cannot go there. *History*, as the word itself implies, is story, narrative claims about the past, that are always descriptive and interpretative, always accounts that are necessarily incomplete and from some point of view. *Heritage* is what we retain from or about the past: our genes, toxic wastes, treasured documents, and preferred historical narratives.

Historical knowledge is an interesting case, because it is so obvious that we are separated from past events and because the significance of traces of the past (old documents, archeological finds, fallible memories) so clearly depend on our interpretations of them. Other areas of knowledge tend to share, in varying degrees, the same attributes: inaccessibility of the object of interest, dependence on interpretation, and, in all cases, interpretations are made within cultural contexts.

Documents as the Activity of Others

Different scholars commonly work on the same topic, or on very closely related topics, at the same time, but not in the same place. When that happens, it would be helpful to come together and share the same space, which would make communication, consultation, and the sharing of notes both convenient and efficient. But a shared workspace is unlikely to be practical for many reasons, even if economic and institutional constraints could be overcome. The other person may be unwilling or unable to move to my space. Even if a prospective collaborator did move into my working area, this approach does not scale, because there may be any number of other prospective collaborators and each of them may want shared space with yet other collaborators who might not be of interest to me. Also, tomorrow I may become more interested in another, different topic and so I want to share my space with some other, different collaborator and, perhaps yet another, different topic and scholar the following day.

There are other difficulties. Even if we know that another scholar shares our interest, we may not know where he is, we may not share a common language, and, in addition to distance as a problem, there is also time. That other scholar may have lost interest in my topic by now. He or she might have died.

As a practical matter, we commune with other scholars through their documents. We deal as best we can with what they wrote and what has been written about their work. Documents become all that survive as means for engaging with that person's ideas and work. Just as our technology incorporates achievements of past inventors, in a similar way we can say that documents embody, selectively and imperfectly, the work and ideas of earlier scholars.

The Social and the Individual

Documents are widely and rightly seen as social, as is reflected in writings on "the social life" of documents and in documents being defined as "social objects." The social role of documents was stressed in our first chapter. But the use of documents can be strictly private and personal, as in the case of a private diary, reading for our own enjoyment, or making private personal notes of some sort that are not intended for other individuals to see and who might not understand them if they did. Describing documents as social objects is not wrong, but it is incomplete. This could be remedied by changing "social objects" to "cultural objects," since "cultural" includes both individual and group behavior.

Society is composed of individuals and, to be precise, it is individuals, not societies, that interact with documents, even though some processes may be delegated to machines. It is individuals who create documents to achieve some end and whose perceptions and misperceptions of documents have cognitive and emotional consequences. Two or more individuals may well collaborate in the creation or revision of documents, and two or more individuals might react to a document in the same way, but they are still individuals. Nevertheless, the individual use of documents is ordinarily social because it is cultural, and we are, or should be, concerned with who originated and who may see any document.

Physical, Mental, and Social Dimensions of Information

It will be clear by now that information has physical, mental, and social aspects. Here, we review these three dimensions and note some relationships between them.

The Physical

A document is something regarded by someone as signifying something. It has to be a physical, material entity unless and until we want to expand into extrasensory perception, direct divine inspiration, or telepathy. It is sometimes assumed or implied that electronic records ("the virtual") are somehow not physical, but this is an error because electronic systems are physical. They do not achieve much without, for example, magnetic charges or electrical power.

One can discuss a *text* or a *work* in an abstract sense, but texts and works can exist as documents only in some physical manifestation. Information systems are supposed to inform people, but this is always and only through physical stuff. All engineered information systems operate on physical records, whether print on paper, holes in a punch card, magnetized bits, optical pulses, or other physical media.

The physical aspect means that all documents exist in space and time. The spatial aspect means that all documents occupy physical space somewhere, and anything existing in physical space can, in principle, be moved to a new location, though ease of mobility varies greatly. The temporal aspect of documents is also important. It may take time to read a text or hear a recording. Some kinds of documents are designed to change over time, for example movies and other performances.

And, as time passes, anything physical will eventually change, making stability and preservation important practical issues. An extreme case is the vulnerability of electronic records to loss or corruption. The history of document technology—writing, printing, telecommunications, copying—can be seen as a continuing effort to reduce the constraints of time and place.

The Mental

The physical dimension is a necessary but not a sufficient condition for being a document. Someone must view it as signifying (or potentially signifying) something, even if they are unsure of what the significance might be. Suzanne Briet, in her explanation of documents and documentation, stated that a document constitutes evidence: "A document is proof in support of a fact" (1951/2006, 9). Her original used the French word *preuve*, which corresponds to the English *proof*, but can also refer to testimony and evidence.

Status as a document (as actually or potentially evidence of something) is an individual, personal mental judgment and, therefore, subjective. Such a perception occurs only in a living mind and, with any living, learning mind, the perception can change when what the individual knows changes, as it does continually until death. Although the consequences of this perception might be observable, the perception itself is neither observable nor measurable.

The Social

The adjective "social" is widely used in relation to documents. We read about "the social life of documents" (e.g., Brown and Duguid 2000) or of documents as "social traces" (e.g., Ferraris 2013). But if we assume that only an individual can be informed by a document (through a mental construction), then caution is needed to distinguish the social from the mental. If we set aside the use of *social* when used figuratively to denote a multiplicity of individuals engaged in subjective mental activity as belonging more properly to the *mental* aspect, the *social* can include the sociology of knowledge, especially interactions between two or more different individuals influencing each other in their understanding of reality.

In their *The Social Construction of Reality: A Treatise in the Sociology of Knowledge* (1966), Berger and Luckmann provide a detailed explanation of how the subjective can be made objective, and thereby accessible to others, through an expression (a frown), a gesture (with a dagger), or a conversation. They rightly emphasize the power of language, but in doing so an opportunity was lost in what could have been added. Language, a most important ingredient in communication, is largely and increasingly expressed in documents. Had that point been made, the study of documents and of documentation might have received much more attention in the past half-century.

A central concept in the sociology of knowledge is *intersubjectivity*. An individual can make a subjective idea objectively perceptible by others. For example, a hostile attitude may be made objective by a frown, by the threatening use of a weapon, or by using angry words, to another individual, who then makes a subjective interpretation and reacts and responds accordingly. In this way, subjective understandings develop among two or more individuals in a related, dialectic way. These more or less shared subjective understandings–*intersubjective* understandings—form the basis of the shared culture of any social group. These are still individual subjective understandings, but they become shared, and are in that sense social.

The social dimension is reflected in collaborative actions, such as teamwork and coercion. The multiplicity, complexity, and fluidity of social groupings should be noted.

Physical and Social Dimensions

All communities depend on the division of labor, resulting in a social division of specialized knowledge and, increasingly, members' dependence on secondhand knowledge. It is the rise of physical documentary techniques such as writing, printing, telecommunications, copying, and computing that has enabled the social division of labor and what is ordinarily meant by "information society."

A text may be authored through the mental efforts of a solitary individual, but physical documents are ordinarily the result of the actions of many different people. A printed book depends on paper manufacturers, printers, publishers, typesetters, binders, book retailers, and many others. Shared financial, transportation, and other infrastructures support all of their varied contributions, and a book would not be printed in the absence of readers.

The social and the physical combine in ways that involve the mental dimension less directly in the area of information policy in which social powers are used to enable or, commonly, to restrict mental activity through economic, legislative, political, and other means. Examples include the regulations governing intellectual property,

It is the rise of physical documentary techniques such as writing, printing, telecommunications, copying, and computing that has enabled the social division of labor and what is ordinarily meant by "information society."

textbook adoption, privacy, libel, technical standards, and national security. These affordances influence mental activity indirectly by influencing the opportunities.

Social and Mental Dimensions

Behavior derives from both nature and nurture. Our mental behavior is profoundly influenced by nurture, by what we learn directly or indirectly from others. Nurture is a social process. Our culture and cultural heritage are socially derived. As Fleck emphasized, understanding a written text requires taking into account the writer's cultural context. In terms of our present discussion, a document must have both physical and mental properties, but since the mental processes are culturally entangled with the social, the status of being a document necessarily also entails a social dimension indirectly through the mental. This alone is sufficient justification for believing every document must necessarily have a social angle as well as mental and physical angles.

Physical, Mental, and Social Dimensions

We have so far focused on pairs of dimensions, but it can be noticed that the third dimension sooner or later emerges as implicated. We use, and need to use, documents to aid, to persuade, to control, and in many other ways, and in doing so the three angles—the social, the physical and the mental—are all directly in use.

Summary

Individuals use documents in varied ways: to learn, verify, communicate, record, enjoy, monitor, and avoid what they do not want. Much of our interaction with others is through messages and other documents. How we use them and how we understand them are parts of our culture. We each live in small but complex worlds, and our writing, reading, and understanding all occur within our cultural contexts; even facts need to be understood in context.

In the next chapter, we look at how documents are organized through arrangement and description.

ORGANIZING:
ARRANGEMENT AND DESCRIPTION

We have noted the vast increase in records of every kind, but very few of them are likely to be of importance for any one person at any given time, so two challenges result: how are we to discover among the very many unknown documents which, if any, are important for us for some purpose, and how are we to find a copy of any identified wanted document? The "information explosion" would not matter if we always had at hand the most suitable documents whenever we wanted or needed them, but that is most unlikely. We need to find them, and finding them is practical only if they have been arranged in some suitably useful way. Finding a copy of an already identified document is a practical, technical task. Discovering *which* documents would be most suitable for us is a different and bigger challenge. Ordinarily this is done in two stages: the formation of collections and then searching within then.

The "information explosion" would not matter if we always had at hand the most suitable documents whenever we wanted or needed them, but that is most unlikely.

Collecting is necessary for preservation as well as use. Organizing a collection becomes more difficult with scale. With one or a few items, no organizing is needed, but as the number increases to hundreds or thousands, remembering each one and where it is quickly becomes impractical. This challenge is addressed through the complementary procedures of description and arrangement, or what can be informally called marking and parking. Describing can be difficult and can never anticipate all future needs. The basic mechanism for organization is matching: assigning descriptions to documents and matching queries with the descriptions.

Collections

We collect what we want, based on some combination of expected value in use and the likelihood of our ever needing it. Collections serve four quite different purposes.

1. Preserving

Unless at least one copy of a record is kept, evidence is lost. The last copy of anything is usually an irreplaceable resource, so it is prudent to retain it even if future use is not expected. There have been regrettable losses. Many ancient Greek plays and many early silent films have not survived. Records are needed, too, for practical reasons such as justifying tax claims. And who has never regretted the failure to back up a computer file?

2. Dispensing and Demand

A quite different reason for collecting is that, although we usually do not know with certainty when or how often an item will be wanted, we can, more or less, predict and act accordingly. The primary benefit of collections lies in their use, so, unless we do not want this use to occur, the more closely a collection matches the pattern of demand (as compatible with the purposes of the collection owner), the greater the benefit.

The difference between preserving and dispensing is very clear in libraries' collections of printed books. No two library collections are ever exactly the same, but, by and large, libraries with similar missions (e.g., university libraries or municipal public libraries) will tend to develop similar collections because they serve communities with similar interests. This is appropriate, because with printed books having a copy available in a local collection dominates the quality of service. If, nationwide, only two or three copies of each edition were retained as preservation copies and all other copies were destroyed, the great majority of volumes in libraries' collections would disappear and libraries would fail in their mission.

3. Display

Sometimes it is helpful to retain a representative sample for explanatory purposes more or less independently of expressed demand. Sales catalogs show most or all of a retailer's offerings. Museums like to have representative examples of a variety of schools of art or of animal species. Librarians consciously seek to offer "balanced" collections on their shelves in order that readers become aware of books and viewpoints new to them or at which they might not ordinarily look.

4. Assets

Collection behavior cannot be fully explained by the preserving, dispensing, and display roles. A collection can also be viewed as an asset. Exceptionally complete library or museum collections bring prestige to their institutions even if the high cost is not compensated by use. In other cases, collected assets such as scanned books, music recordings, or records of sales transactions or traffic patterns constitute an asset that might support strategic insights or yield revenue through sales or services.

These four roles of collections are not independent of each other. They compete for investment, and they can be in conflict in other ways also. The dispensing role is designed for use but use is harmful to preservation. Library collection development policy is ordinarily seen as a trade-off between the dispensing role (catering to expected demand) and the display role (providing materials deemed by the librarians to be good for the users). The latter may seem paternalistic. It is. It reflects the mission of the library service to promote an improved community made more aware of available choices. In library terms where collecting is done to benefit others, this becomes a compromise between what would be valuable for readers and what library users will demand.

Arrangement and Lists

Inevitably, as the number of documents has increased, efforts to arrange and to describe them have become pervasive, and many different names have been used to denote their management (selection, collection, arrangement, indexing, etc.). Bibliography, documentation, and information science have each been used to describe the field in a broad sense, and numerous other terms have been used for specialized areas.

We can arrange collected documents, but one single arrangement will not suit all needs. Arrangement by topic hinders search by author, and vice versa. The practical solution is to arrange brief representations of documents in multiple additional arrangements. Differently stated, we can create multiple indexes to the collection. Each index (list) is itself also a collection, a collection of descriptions of documents.

Listed documents can be arranged in different ways: by author, by date, by title, by topic, and so on. So listing allows economically for multiple alternative arrangements of multiple representations. A traditional name for this is activity is bibliography. We ordinarily think of a bibliography as a list, but a list can be arranged in complex ways.

Organizing a collection becomes more difficult with scale. With one or a few items, no organizing is needed, but as the number increases to hundreds or thousands, remembering each one and where it is quickly becomes impractical without a purposeful, systematic arrangement. You might need to examine every single one to be sure that you have found the best one. If we expand the number to millions, the difficulty is obvious. This challenge is addressed through arrangement and description.

Description

Documents ordinarily need description, because a document's characteristics may not be self-evident from looking at it, because the document may not be readily visible, and because added description provides a better basis for selection. For example, one cannot know from looking at a book that a later, more up-to-date edition has appeared, but a description could include a note saying so, and similar descriptions can be used to relate similar documents to each other. A common general term for these descriptions is *metadata*, meaning data about a document or, more generally, data about data.

Librarians make descriptions of documents in their catalogs and through classified arrangements on their shelves. In all contexts, assigning topic names to documents and assigning documents to named topic categories is central. In Robert Fairthorne's colorful terms:

> All retrieval systems demand marks of some kind. …
> An object can be marked by changing it intrinsically
> in some recognizable way—as by painting it,
> punching a hole, or introducing it to a skunk. This I
> call "inscribing."
>
> Or it can be changed relative to its environment by
> putting it upside down, on one side, in an inscribed
> pigeon-hole, and so forth. This I call "ordering" the
> item. Better terms for less formal contexts are
> "marking" and "parking." (Fairthorne 1961,
> 84–85)

Names (marks) are essential for the use of collections. They are, necessarily, linguistic expressions and, as we shall see, they create tensions and difficulties beyond our control.

Descriptions of documents serve three functions.

1. They characterize the document, telling us what kind of a document it is, what it is about, where it came from, and so on.

2. They may also represent a document, serving as a substitute for it that may sometimes be sufficient for some purposes. For example, an entry in a bibliography or in a library catalog may be sufficient to verify an incomplete citation.

3. They also show relationships between documents. If both of two documents are described as having the same author, then these two documents are related by shared authorship. If two documents are both described as being about, say, Malta, then they are related in subject matter; and so on. Traditionally, items with shared characteristics are described as *sets*. Increasingly, relationships between them are described as *networks* or *graphs* and shared characteristics as *links*.

The purpose of description is to enable identification and selection. Since selection will depend on the purpose of use, and not all purposes are fully predictable, description practices have to be a trade-off between the purposes the description is intended to support, the expected pattern of use, and costs. The following are important requirements for description:

The purpose of description is to enable identification and selection.

1. description of the significance of a document as evidence. What is the text, data set, or object about? What does the text discuss? What do the data depict? What does the object show? Who created it? What is it good for? For what imagined need has it been included in the collection?

2. physical description of the document. What physical medium is it—printed book, digital text file, biological specimen? Specific details are likely to be useful: in 24 volumes, an Excel spreadsheet, dried pressed plants, oil painting in canvas, etc. What is its origin, lineage, and version? What is its physical condition?

3. administrative practicalities. Where is a copy currently located? What are the conditions of use? Who has ownership rights to the object or intellectual property rights to it?

The sum of the descriptions (the "metadata") will be discussed further in chapter 7.

Not So Easy!

Two examples can illustrate the tasks of arrangement and description.

Arranging Coins

Suppose we had a box of foreign coins, old and new. How might we arrange them? An obvious practical start would be to sort them by the country that issued them. A different, useful division would be between coins that are still legal tender and those that are not. Adoption of the euro displaced numerous national currencies.

Another practical plan would be to separate the coins that have value to collectors, if we know which they are. Those that do should also be categorized by condition ("mint," "fine," etc.). Other plausible arrangements would be by weight, by size, by thickness, by date of issue, date collected, or by the metal they are made of.

Visual bases for arrangement include shape. Not all coins are round, some have holes, some have milled edges, others do not. Many coins have portraits, some of living persons, some of dead, and some of mythical, symbolic persons. Many depict animals or plants. One could also sort by the script or language of the writing on them. Many more ways to arrange coins are imaginable, but these are enough to draw the following conclusions.

1.   We need to choose an arrangement. The coins themselves are not easily arranged in more than one way at a time, and rearranging them would be tedious.

2.   Descriptions of the coins, however, are much more easily arranged in multiple ways. The coins themselves

could be arranged in the order acquired or even randomly, and descriptions of each coin could be multiplied inexpensively for as many different arrangements as desired, with each description used for a different arrangement and each one with a pointer to the location of the original coin for whenever the description itself is not enough or inspection of the coin itself is necessary. This is how libraries work—books are usually shelved according to a subject classification order, and entries are made in the catalog for other useful arrangements: one for each author of each book, another for each title, and more for subject headings. On each catalog record is the call number indicating the book's location on the shelves. This is obviously less costly than acquiring additional copies of each book to create additional arrangement of books by author, by title, and by subject heading, or rearranging the books themselves when a different ordering is desired.

3.   We need to be selective. Every added detail of description and each arrangement requires effort, and not all arrangements are likely to be equally useful. It depends on the *purpose* of the collection and the most important wants and needs of whoever will use the collection. If an important but unforeseen principle of arrangement is wanted—all coins with portraits of women, perhaps—the entire collection could still be searched one by one.

4.   We never know enough. We cannot be sure that we know what arrangements may be needed in the future. We may not know what the metal is, perhaps an alloy, or that an author's name may be a pseudonym. Maybe we are unsure whether a metal token really should be considered a coin.

Describing People

Our discussion of coins focused on arrangement. To illustrate difficulties of description, consider the design of a database of people for a dating or a matchmaking service. Some elements are relatively straightforward: age, gender, address, height, and occupation, if any. But these attributes are not likely to be sufficient or, even, the most important. An inquirer will want to know whether this prospective mate has a sympathetic personality, a sense of humor, emotional stability, and compatible spirituality. How are we to define, represent, and calibrate these qualities? How confident can we be in our assessments? In this example, it seems that the more important the attribute, the more difficult it is to express a useful value. And how important are these different attributes relative to each other? Each human candidate is a complicated combination of complex qualities.

Arrangement and description involve different processes and different results. One could assign the description "subject: economics" to each book on that topic, or we could place all books on economics in a shelf labeled "economics." But the practical effect is essentially the same. In this sense, arrangement and description are functionally the same and in principle interchangeable. In the first case, the description follows whatever arrangement the books happen to be in. In the second case, the relationship is inverted: the books—or, at least, pointers to them—are arranged in whatever order the descriptions are in.

Generating Descriptions

Because of the practical difficulties of description, all implemented systems of arrangement and description will always be to some extent incomplete or imperfect for searchers. Whatever the decisions and difficulties, the result emerges in the following general form: an object (e.g., a coin) has an attribute (e.g., weight) with some value (e.g., 5 grams). For example:

Object	Attribute	Value
Person	Age	45
Book	Topic	Economics
House	Bedrooms	3

Given the cost and difficulties of describing, it would be convenient if documents could describe themselves, and the more so as the number of documents to be described increases. In practice, this is a matter of drawing mechanically on the physical aspects of documents. Text documents lend themselves to this approach, because words in the text reflect what the text discusses. For large text files, and especially on the web, this becomes the only affordable approach and is the basic mechanism of web search services, as described in chapter 7.

This concordance approach to searching text is extremely economical, but it has some weaknesses. The words are simply treated as a string of characters, so no meaning is involved. Words that are spelled the same but have different meanings (homographs), like *bank* (financial institution) and *bank* (river side) and *bank* (tilt when turning), are the same string of characters and so are not distinguished. And different words with the same meaning (synonyms, such as *fiddle* and *violin*) are not connected. So some irrelevant documents may be retrieved, and some relevant documents may not be retrieved. Several refinements are possible. A "stop list" of words not expected to be useful (e.g., *a*, *the*) are not indexed. Measures can be taken to connect differently spelled words with the same meaning (synonyms), to distinguish different meanings of the words that are spelled the same (homographs), to correct misspellings, and, more ambitiously, to show different but similar or related words.

Most selection systems are designed to retrieve all documents that match a query, but searchers rarely want all of them. Commonly *any one* document that matches is enough, or *a few* or *the most recent* or *the earliest*. In general, whatever the query and whatever the collection, supplying a small number of the *least unsuitable* would be best.

The Basic Mechanism

The basic mechanism is simple. Indexes work by reversing ("inverting") the object-attribute-value relationship. Instead of a subject descriptor being attached to the document, the document is attached to the subject descriptor. For example, if Book$_1$ has the subject "economics"; Book$_2$ has the subject "elephants," and Book$_3$ also has the subject "elephants," then, if we reverse these statements, "economics" leads to Book$_1$ and "elephants" leads to Book$_2$ and Book$_3$.

Queries

A searcher needs to express a *query,* which needs to lead to an *index entry,* which leads to a book. For example,

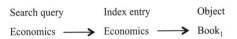

Search query   Index entry   Object

Economics ⟶ Economics ⟶ Book$_1$

Figure 1   Query, description, and object.

More generally,

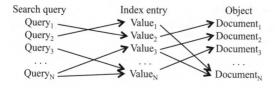

Figure 2 Multiple links matching queries to index entries and index entries to documents.

There are, of course, some consequences: for success, each query needs to connect to at least one index entry, and each index entry needs to connect to at least one suitable document if anything is to be found.

Summary

The problem of discovering documents we need and of getting a copy when needed is handled by forming collections, making descriptions, and using arrangements: marking and parking. Lists are virtual collections. Successful search depends on how suitable the descriptions and arrangements are for purposes of the search. Describing is a language act, which we examine in the next chapter. In the following chapters, we discuss the organizing of descriptions, matching techniques, and the evaluation of search results.

NAMING

Finding operations depend heavily on the names assigned to document descriptions and on the named categories to which documents are assigned. Naming is a language activity, and so inherently a cultural activity. Here we provide a brief introduction to the issues, tensions, and compromises involved in describing collected documents. The notation can be codes or ordinary words. Search will be more reliable if related words are linked. Combinations of terms will be needed for complex topics, and the amount of detail needed varies with the situation. Naming draws on already established terminology for future searching, but problems arise because language continually changes and because new concepts need new names, which are often, at first, unreliable. Systems can only work on physical marks—in effect, on mentions, not meanings. Because language is cultural, changes in culture can affect the acceptability of names as well as their meaning.

Topic Descriptions

Once collected, documents have to be made accessible in an organized way. Librarians, for example, make descriptions of documents in their catalogs and also through classified subject arrangements on their shelves. Assigning topic names to documents and assigning documents to named topical categories are central.

Names (marks) are essential for collected documents to be findable. Names are, necessarily, linguistic expressions and—as we shall see—they create tensions and difficulties. Libraries are cultural institutions concerned with recorded knowledge, and their mission is to support learning, both research (knowing more) and teaching (sharing understanding). Libraries exist to advance learning, knowledge, understanding, and belief. But what people know, what they would like to know, and what others have learned and written about, all resist mechanical treatment. If it were otherwise, knowledge management could be reduced to data processing.

Searchers seeking documents relevant to their interests have to locate what they need on the system's terms. There is, or should be, collaboration with information service providers seeking to anticipate their users' interests and vocabulary, and users trying to make sense of the category names in the catalog, classification, or bibliography being used. Even if a limited vocabulary or an artificial notation, such as the Dewey Decimal Classification system, is used, all description is a language activity. Description is always and necessarily based in culture, because descriptions are based on the concepts, definitions, and understandings that have developed in a community.

This naming (bibliographic description) follows rules. For more than a century, there has been gradual international standardization of rules for representing the imprint (where and by whom published), collation (physical features of a document), proper names (authors, institutions, and places), and other attributes of documents. The real difficulty, however, for both librarians and library users is in describing what a document is about, in naming its topic, which is usually presented as a two-stage process: first, the cataloger examines a document to determine what concepts it is about; then he or she assigns terms (linguistic expressions) from a vocabulary to denote those concepts. The literature has little to say about the first stage and concentrates on the second. Research has revealed that different indexers will commonly assign different index terms to the same document, as will a single indexer at different times.

Documentary Languages for Naming Topics

There are a variety of methods for representing what documents are about: subject classifications, lists of subject headings, thesauri, ontologies, and so on. A traditional collective term for all of them is *documentary languages*. We need not examine each type, but will note four dimensions along which they vary.

Notation

Verbal approaches using natural language words are a simple and popular way to create descriptions. However, using ordinary vocabulary has disadvantages, and ease of creation does not lead to effective use. The multiplicity and fluidity of natural language vocabulary makes for unpredictable results: should I look under *violin* or *fiddle*, or both? The variations of natural language can be mitigated by adopting a restricted ("controlled") vocabulary, as explained below.

Natural language words do not arrange themselves in a helpful way. Alphabetical filing order is determined by accidents of spelling rather than related meanings. "If the names of the classes, in a natural language, are used to arrange them, we do not get a helpful order. In fact names scatter classes in a most unhelpful chaotic order. It will give us an order like algebra, anger, apple, arrogance, asphalt, and astronomy," wrote the Indian librarian, S. R.

Ranganathan (1951, 34). Also, natural language indexes are ordinarily created only in a single language.

Both of these problems can be addressed by using an artificial notation for the descriptive names (such as the Dewey Decimal Classification) designed to achieve some desired arrangement, with natural language indexes leading to the class numbers in as many different natural languages as desired. Having an artificial notation of letters, numerals, and other symbols does not mean that it is no longer a language. It is an artificial language and is not immune to the problems of obsolescence and perspective discussed below. It is the same approach as the artificially constructed, restricted languages used, for example, in botanical and chemical nomenclature.

Vocabulary Control

Everyday language is characterized by multiplicity, such as singular and plural forms, variant spellings, or synonyms and antonyms (opposites). The same topic could be assigned any number of names, or represented in an indefinite number of ways ("unlimited semiosis"), so documents on the same topic could be scattered under any of several different headings. A searcher might find some but not others. The standard solution is "vocabulary control," whereby one form of name, for example, *violins*, is "preferred," and used exclusively. Other commonly used but "nonpreferred" terms are listed, but only to redirect the searcher to the preferred term: for example, *fiddles, see violins.* An "authority file," a list of the carefully differentiated preferred and nonpreferred terms, is compiled and followed.

Vocabulary control can take care of synonyms, near-synonyms, antonyms, and variant spellings. Exact synonyms are quite rare. It is near-synonyms that are frequent. *Birds* and *ornithology*, for example, are closely related but not quite the same. Even so, someone interested in birds might look under *ornithology* and vice versa. Near-synonyms require endless situational judgments concerning what to combine and what to keep separate.

In practice, vocabulary control also extends to hierarchical and other relationships ("see also"). Vocabulary control extends beyond semantic to functional relationships, which differentiates this kind of word list from traditional dictionaries. *Biogas*, *pig manure,* and *water hyacinths*, for example, are very different from each other, but since pig manure and water hyacinths are important ingredients in making biogas anybody interested in one is likely to be interested in the others. Thus, *see also* references in both directions between each and *biogas* are justifiable.

Coordination

Many documents are concerned with complex topics, needing at least a phrase to express the scope. A simple approach is to simply list the terms, in any order, needed to comprise the meaning. Documents about the "Parents of handicapped children" would have three terms: the three keywords *children* and *handicapped* and *parents*. There are also some documents on "children of handicapped parents," which would also be retrieved by the same keywords, but, being relatively few, would probably not be noticed in the retrieved set. Computers can easily handle keyword searches, but the earlier technology of catalog cards cannot: any such combination has to be "pre-coordinated" using some syntax at the time of cataloging to differentiate and to express relationships among the terms. The US Library of Congress subject headings have two quite separate headings, *children of handicapped parents* and *parents of handicapped children*, which, because they constitute grammatical phrases, are not confused by human searchers. This is a simple case. Syntactic rules are used to generate quite elaborate headings in which a primary term is progressively qualified, either as a complex phrase, such as *hand-to-hand fighting, oriental, in motion pictures*, or with a chain of qualifying terms, as in *God—knowableness—history of doctrines—early church, ca. 30–600—congresses*. The latter is a single subject heading in which the grammar is expressed by the positioning of the terms. For an English speaker accustomed to adjectives preceding the nouns they qualify, it sounds more natural if such headings are read in a reverse order, with some conjunctions and prepositions added: "Congresses on the history of doctrines in the early church, ca 30-600, concerning the knowableness of God." Fortunately, the use of numbers and letters in the artificial notation of classification schemes allows elaborately coordinated topics to be expressed much more concisely. In this way, all but the simplest documentary languages for naming topics have grammar and well as a vocabulary.

Fineness

A collection composed of one or very few documents needs no catalog. At the other extreme, distinguishing every little nicety in order to differentiate every topic becomes cumbersome. Collections of millions do need very detailed description in order to achieve the fineness of sifting required to select a handful rather than a flood of records. In practice, the level of detail in subject indexing is situational, depending on how many different items are acquired in each topic.

Time and Naming

Naming Is Forward-Looking

Subject indexing can be formulated as a matter of fitting descriptions. The challenge is to create descriptions that will enable those to be served to identify and select the best documentary means to whatever their ends may be.

By definition, the descriptions used by indexers are for future use. This requires thinking about likely needs and describing (naming) in a forward-looking way. To do this, the indexer constructs, consciously or not, some mental narrative about future use, some story in which the document in hand could be relevant to future needs. It is not simply a matter of what the document is about, but of where it might be useful in an imagined future. Familiarity with the community and its purposes, ways of thinking, and terminology are important requirements for the effective indexer.

Vesa Suominen asked the question, "What is it that makes a good librarian?" Drawing on the ideas of linguist Ferdinand de Saussure, he answered that the task is one of "filling empty space." The good librarian is one who is effective in arranging documents in relation to each need of each library user. That the populations of documents, of library users, and of needs are all very large and quite unstable makes the task more difficult, but does not undermine the principle. Suzanne Briet extended the idea of this forward-looking stance with her image of the librarian as a hunting dog guided by the hunter (researcher), but also prospecting ahead and pointing to prey invisible to the hunter in a dynamic partnership: "Like a hunter's dog—really in front, guided and guiding." ("Comme le chien du chasseur–tout à fait en avant, guidé, guidant.")

Naming Is Backward-Looking

The effort to be forward-looking is, however, affected by the describing (naming) process. Topical description is a matter of naming what a document is about, and describing is a matter of summarizing. Assigning subject headings is an extreme of summarizing what a document is about. But what, actually, is "aboutness" about? Stating that a subject heading represents a topic or a concept is valid, but unhelpful, because saying that merely points to another name and does not explain. An explanation of what a subject heading (and, therefore, a document) is "about" must be derived from the discourse from which the indexing term originates. A subject description assigned to a document says that *this* discourse (document) relates to *that* discourse (literature, discussion, dialogue) which means that the subject description is invariably based in the past. Similarly, library users don't want topics, they want discourse: a statement, a description, an explanation—or, at least, a discussion of whatever they are curious about. Thus, a subject heading expressing a topic derives its importance from past discourse.

Meanings are established by usage and so always draw on the past. The indexer, then, is creating descriptions by drawing on the past, but expressing them with an eye to the future. This Janus-like stance might seem difficult enough in a stable world, but the reality of indexing is made much worse by time, technology, the nature of language, and social change.

Meanings are established by usage and so always draw on the past. The indexer, then, is creating descriptions by drawing on the past, but expressing them with an eye to the future.

Time of Inscription

The indexer's formal act of naming, of recording the topical description of a document or of specifying a relationship between named topics, is necessarily performed at some point in time and inscribed into the apparatus of indexes and catalogs. As time passes, that act recedes from the present into the past. During the same flow of time the prior discourse, from which the choice of name was derived, has continued, evolved, and changed, and indexing practices will evolve with those changes. Also, as the future becomes the present, new futures continue to be foreseen, and the forward-looking perspective would increasingly be related to changed future expectations. However, an assigned name, once inscribed, is fixed. So, with the passing of time, its relationship with both the then-past discourses and also the then-future expected needs drifts away from relevance to the perceptions of an advancing present. Assigned names are, therefore, inherently obsolescent with respect to both the past and the future. Discourses and the indexer flow forward with time, but the assigned names have been inscribed for, and fixed in, a receding past. Because old indexing relates to past situations, updating it is difficult and not generally attempted.

It is not simply that a new document has to be positioned in relation to both past discourse and future needs. Additional complexity arises because there are, of course, not one but many simultaneous communities of discourse.

Figurative Use of Language

New names arise, especially for new topics, through figurative use of language, especially through metaphor. Well-established terms are used figuratively, based on some perceived similarity, for emerging concepts—for example, a computer "mouse." Then, through usage, the new meaning becomes fixed, at first within its context, then more widely. The instability of language is not of the indexer's making. Indexers must follow changes in word usage. They take a conservative approach because changes in terminology call into question older terminology, and the task of making retroactive alterations to the marks in an index takes resources away from other worthy purposes.

Mention and Meaning

Information services depend heavily on technology. Documents are physical objects on paper, film, magnetic disk, or other physical media. Libraries could not operate as they do if the tasks to be performed were not heavily routinized and most of them reduced to clerical procedures performed by support staff or delegated to machines. The modern library arose in the spirit of late nineteenth-century technological modernism as "library economy," imbued by Melvil Dewey and others with an emphasis on standards, system, efficiency, and collective progress that lives on in visions of digital libraries, the "semantic web," and the "virtual." Detailed control is needed for effectiveness and for efficiency, and librarians, pioneers of new technology for filing and record processing, inspired modern office-management procedures.

In subject indexing, the machinic and the cultural collide like two tectonic plates, and naming lies at the fault line where indexers use vocabulary control to try to mitigate the linguistic ruptures and slidings they can neither prevent nor avoid. Thus, there is an endemic battle between the incorrigibly cultural and aesthetic character of the underlying mission and the machinic tendencies essential for cost-effective performance. The central battle line of these tensions is in naming what documents are about.

The fact that the documents are overwhelmingly textual has allowed the heavy use of natural language processing techniques to infer semantic relationships between documents and between documents and queries. But this is a matter of lexical entities, of character strings, not of meanings. Fairthorne (1961) analyzed this difference by saying that these techniques deal with mentions, not meanings. For example, if *information* and *retrieval* commonly co-occur in that order, then they are presumed to constitute a phrase. And if the phrase *information retrieval* and the phrase *vector space* tend to co-occur in the same texts, they are computed as being close in "document space," and a topical relationship is inferred from this "spatial" proximity. If relationships between marks are statistically significant, semantic affinities are implied but not explained. Machines can be programmed to detect regularities and inconsistencies among marks, even if they cannot distinguish sense from nonsense.

It is further evidence of the inherently linguistic character of bibliographical access that formulaic natural language processing techniques work quite well, but not always and not very reliably. It is the textual (lexical) similarity between documents that allows relatedness between discourses and descriptions to be inferred, since the same words are mentioned when the same or very similar language is in use. From the method employed, homographs with different meanings—for example, *host* (landlord) and *host* (crowd)—will dilute the precision of retrieval. The compelling economic attraction of this approach is, of course, that it is mechanical and so can be delegated to machines. The poverty of this approach arises when different vocabularies are used to refer to the same topic without using (mentioning) the same terms. For this and for cross-lingual search, formal structures such as bilingual dictionaries or statistical associations help. The important and useful specialized vocabularies relating to places, events, and persons, which are partly cultural and partly physical, will be discussed in the next chapter.

Technical writing on information retrieval draws heavily on natural language processing to identify personal and institutional names and many types of frequency counts and statistical associations. This needs to be complemented by attention to the way that words are used and the unlimited number of ways of saying something (Blair 1990). Both categories and the language used to label them are deeply subjective (e.g., Lakoff 1987). Research on the social practices of science is contributing to understanding the use and role of documents and document description (e.g., Frohmann 2004). *Sorting Things Out: Classification and its Consequences* by Geoffrey Bowker and Susan Leigh Star (1999) provides revealing case studies of how social agendas influence the design of supposedly objective categorization systems.

Naming Is Cultural

Language evolves within communities of discourse and produces and evokes those communities. Every such community has its own more or less specialized, stylized practice of language. Attempts at controlled or stabilized vocabulary must deal with multiple and dynamic discourses and the resulting multiplicity and instability of meanings. Most bibliographies and catalogs have a single topical index, but include material of interest to more than one community. Since each community has slightly different linguistic practices, no one index will be ideal for everyone and, perhaps, not for anyone. In vernacular discussion of health, for example, the terms *cancer* and *stroke* are commonly used, but in professional medical writing *neoplasm* and *cerebrovascular accident* are preferred names. So, in theory, multiple, dynamic indexes, one for each community, would be ideal. It is not, however, only a matter of linguistic variation, but also of perspective. Different discourses discuss different issues or, when the same issue, from different perspectives. A *rabbit* can be discussed as a pet, as a pest, as food, or as a character in a book.

Aside from these "dialect" differences, the vocabulary used by indexers to characterize their documents can become problematic for other reasons as the world changes. There are cognitive developments: new ideas and new inventions need new names. *Horseless carriages* were invented, then renamed *automobiles*. Also, new referents emerge for existing names. Some sixty years ago the word *computer* meant a human who performed calculations, but now always means a machine. More recently, the word *printer* made the same transition.

Fighting Words

There are also consequences for library naming from affective changes. Even when the meaning (denotation) is stable, the associated context (connotation) or attitudes to what is referred to may change. Always, some linguistic expressions are socially unacceptable. That might not matter much, except that what is deemed acceptable or unacceptable not only differs from one cultural group to another, but changes over time, and, especially during changes, may be unpleasantly controversial. The phrase *yellow peril* was once widely used to denote what was seen as excessive immigration from the Far East, but it is now considered too offensive to use, even though there is no convenient and acceptable replacement term for this view and the phrase *yellow peril* is needed in historical discussion.

Much has been written concerning the social acceptability of subject headings, both the terms used and how they are related to each other. "*Sexual perversion* see also *Homosexuality*" was once, but is now no longer, acceptable. Sanford Berman's *Prejudices and Antipathies: A Tract on the LC Subject Heads Concerning People* (1971) is an excellent introduction. Berman picks out scores of subject headings, explains why each is, in his opinion, offensive, and recommends alternative terms he considers more acceptable. His examples and commentary show how naming always reflects a cultural perspective, that terminology acceptable to one group may be offensive to another, and that attitudes change over time. For example, *Jewish question* implies untenable assumptions; *Gypsies* are not from Egypt and prefer to be called *Roma*; the cross-reference "*Rogues and vagabonds* see also *Gypsies*" exhibits prejudice; the headings *Mammies* and *Negroes* are offensive to those so named; *Eskimos* are properly called *Inuit*; and so on. His examples are far too many and too interesting to summarize here.

One's own behavior is reflected as superior to that of others: rebellions by slaves are named *insurrections*, but rebellions by citizens are more positively named *revolutions*. *Indians of North America, Civilization of* did not refer to the culture of Native Americans, but to progress in the eradication of their culture and its replacement with European settlers' lifestyle, as the Library of Congress instruction made clear: "Here is entered literature dealing with efforts to civilize the Indians." European powers have colonies; the United States has offshore "territories and possessions" not called colonies. Many of Berman's examples reflect a male and Christian world view, the social attitudes of past times, and obsolete medical and psychological terminology (e.g., *Idiocy*). In some cases, counterarguments can be made. For example, using *Roma* for Gypsies is counterproductive or inefficient if the library's users are unfamiliar with that term.

Tracing shifts in subject indexing back through time is an instructive form of cultural and linguistic archeology. The *Library of Congress Subject Headings* is more than a hundred years old, has well over a hundred thousand different headings, and is difficult to update. It is an easy target in spite of many reforms, and a good example of a problem that is endemic in indexes and categorization systems. Linguistic expressions are necessarily culturally grounded and so unstable and, for that reason, are in conflict with the need to have stable, unambiguous marks if systems are to perform efficiently.

In addition to the problems of naming, much of the naming is of concepts that are themselves abstract or problematic, and there is no linguistic solution for conceptual vagueness or confusion.

Summary

Describing is a matter of naming characteristics of documents, especially what they are about. Descriptions vary by notation (words or codes), vocabulary control (standardized terminology), coordination of combinations for complex topics (e.g., venetian blind), and fineness (how detailed). Describing is a language activity drawing on already established terminology for future searches, but since language evolves, descriptions are necessarily obsolescent. Because language is cultural, descriptions of sensitive topics may be contested. The next chapter will examine in more detail how descriptions are organized and used.

Linguistic expressions are necessarily culturally grounded and so unstable and, for that reason, are in conflict with the need to have stable, unambiguous marks if systems are to perform efficiently.

METADATA

Having looked at how naming is used in describing, we now examine how descriptions are used. *Metadata* (literally beyond or with data) is a common name for descriptions of documents, records, and data: it is data about data. Here we do not distinguish between *data* and *documents*. The first and most obvious use of metadata is description, but inverting the relationship so that description becomes central rather than peripheral enables metadata to also serve as the preferred basis for search and discovery. However, depending on metadata for search also runs into difficulties caused by differing vocabularies used in different contexts, the unlimited variety and instability of language, and the need to relate different but comparable terms and to distinguish different uses of the same words. It is useful to distinguish fundamentally different aspects

Metadata (literally beyond or with data) is a common name for descriptions of documents, records, and data: it is data about data.

(facets), such as what, where, when, and who, and to treat them separately.

The First Purpose of Metadata: Description

The first and original use of metadata is to describe documents. There are different kinds of descriptive metadata:

technical (to describe format, encoding standards, etc.);

administrative (copyright ownership, conditions of use, etc.); and

content (the subject matter, scope, authorship, etc.).

These descriptions help in understanding a document's character and in deciding whether to make use of it. Description can be very useful, even if nonstandard terminology is used. Almost any description is better than none. However, it is always strongly recommended that descriptive metadata follow standard forms in order to facilitate comparison.

Metadata has two components: a format and a set of values. Well-known formats include XML, the Dublin Core, and MARC (for sharing library catalog records). Each is associated with specific standards for defining the kinds of descriptions that may be used with them.

The use of standardized formats for storing and displaying makes use of metadata easier. Use of standard vocabularies has the advantage of consistency and aids understanding.

When documents are browsed, especially digital documents, descriptive metadata is used to understand what kind of document it is, what it is about, and how to use it. This process resembles the way one can look at the cover of a book to help assess the text inside.

Creating Indexes

To establish a meaningful connection between a query and a document or between two different documents, two actions are required: first, make a connection between them, and then express the nature of the relationship between them. For example, one might assign the same topic description to both, or a subject heading can be assigned to a text and the same subject heading also assigned to an image, as shown in figure 3.

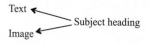

Figure 3   Subject heading assigned to a text and to an image.

The next step is to invert this relationship, so that one can go from the subject heading both to the text and also to the image. This allows a unified search of both texts and images relating to the same topic, starting with a query leading to a subject heading (value) leading to documents, as discussed in chapter 5 and shown in figure 4.

Figure 4   A subject leading to a text and to an image.

This maneuver inverts the original structure. Instead of descriptions being attached to documents, the documents are attached to the descriptions. The vocabulary of the descriptions becomes primary, and the documents become peripheral. This inversion is clearly seen in citation indexes. When you examine books and articles, the references are peripheral, in footnotes or at the end, and are often in smaller type. But a citation index inverts that relationship. The citations themselves and the relationships between them become primary. Only when a citation of interest has been selected is a document, at the periphery, consulted.

This relationship also allows a transverse search from a text through a subject heading to an image assigned the same subject heading, or, equally, from an image to texts, as shown in figure 5.

Text ⟷ Subject heading ⟷ Image

Figure 5   A text and an image linked to each other by a subject heading.

In this way, two or more documents on the same topic, however different their format or content, can be related to each other as a network. This process depends on having a single vocabulary to describe topics, or, at least, interoperable vocabularies.

Index Terms

Tagging—inviting anybody to assign any words that seem appropriate—has become popular. This practice is convenient and can be helpful as a starting basis for more formal indexing vocabulary. It can also help identify symbolic and emotional aspects of images and texts. However, best professional indexing practice is based on the following three principles.

Vocabulary control, or limiting the terms used so as to combine synonyms and near-synonyms. In order to remain consistent, it is useful to maintain an "authority list" of the terms used ("preferred terms") as well as the synonyms and near-synonyms ("nonpreferred terms"). Personal names are important for authorship and biographical texts. The need to differentiate between different persons with the same name and aggregating different names for the same person is well understood in archives, libraries, museums, and elsewhere. Proper names pose the difficulty that two different people may have the same name, and the same person may have multiple names during her or his lifetime. The former need to be adequately differentiated, for example by adding birth and death dates. The latter need to be associated and one form consistently used. Similarly, the same place names may occur in multiple locations, and a single place may have multiple names in different languages or change its name over time. Whenever needed, a scope note clarifies the meaning and, in particular, for proper names a source for the choice is cited.

Facet analysis, the initial separation of all index terms into groups that each represent quite different aspects ("facets") of the universe that are different in kind—for example, time, place, and persons. These elements can later be combined to represent complex topics as desired.

A *grammar*, for distinguishing different descriptive phrases that use the same words—for example, "man bites dog" and "dog bites man."

These three techniques permit the development of very precise descriptive systems.

The Second Use of Metadata: Search

Thinking of metadata as a means for describing individual documents reflects only one of the two roles of metadata. The second use of metadata is different: it emerges when you *start* with a query or with the description rather than the document—with the metadata rather than the data— when searching in an index.

This second use of metadata is for finding, for search and discovery. In a digital environment for texts, it is common and convenient to use textual queries and to search for the occurrence of text fragments in the available documents, as web search engines do. So, a search for the topic "mouse" is expressed as the character string "m o u s e," and every document containing that sequence of characters will be retrieved, whether it discusses a small mammal or refers to its (originally figurative) use for a computer input device or other uses of the word. The technique of searching text by character strings works quite well, but not always and not perfectly, because text resources are not entirely homogeneous. Some words have multiple meanings (polysemy); sometimes different words use the same character string but have different meanings (homographs); and different words may be used with the same meaning (synonyms, such as *cancer* and *neoplasm*).

Simple text searches break down in multilingual environments as well as when nontextual resources are included, such as images, sounds, and numeric data sets. An image can be compared with other images, and a sound can be compared with other sounds, but an image cannot be compared directly with a sound or other media forms. One cannot ordinarily use a query composed of a few pixels, or a sound, as a query in a text file. The usual remedy is to add to each nontext object a textual description that can be searched by a textual query.

Infrastructure is a collective term for the subordinate parts of an undertaking. It was initially used to refer to fixed resources used for transportation and military operations and has been gradually extended to include services ancillary to, or in support of, the performance of a central task. Minimally, travel by train requires tracks, a locomotive, and wagons, but an effective and reliable railroad service also depends on other auxiliary resources: systems for signaling, ticketing, communication between stations, fuel supplies, a management structure, publication of timetables, and so on. The collective name for these auxiliary resources is infrastructure.

Infrastructure is always some kind of structure, but which structures should be considered *infra*structure is situational. A bank needs the support of data processing services to provide its banking services, and this computing support is considered part of the bank's infrastructure. For the computer services industry, auxiliary resources—the infrastructure—include reliable banking services for handling payments. So banking services are, in turn, part of the infrastructure of the computer services industry.

Standards and protocols are an intangible form of infrastructure with very tangible consequences. Since infrastructure is considered to be the environment of support that enables and empowers, social conventions and mentalities—the structures of thought discussed in Michel Foucault's *The Order of Things* (1970)—could be considered a form of infrastructure.

To summarize, the first and original use of metadata is for describing documents, and the name *metadata* (beyond or with data) along with its popular definition, "data about data," are based on this use. A second use of metadata is to form organizing structures by means of which documents can be arranged. These structures can be used both to search for individual documents and also to identify patterns within a population of documents. The second role of metadata involves an inversion of the relationship between document and metadata. These structures can be considered infrastructure.

A second use of metadata is to form organizing structures by means of which documents can be arranged.

The remainder of this chapter examines features of metadata when used for search and discovery within a reference work, in a library, or when searching online.

A Multiplicity of (Mostly) Unfamiliar Vocabularies

Since language evolves within cultural contexts, this becomes more marked when one ventures into the indexes of other disciplines, of different media, and of foreign countries. One can search effectively and efficiently only when one dealing with a vocabulary with which one is familiar. How many people know that search terms for *automobiles* should include, among many others, the following?

PASS MOT VEH, SPARK IGN ENG (US Federal Import/Export statistics codes)

TL 205 (Library of Congress classification)

180/280 (US patent classification)

3711 (Standard Industrial Classification)

The whole point of a network environment is to make more and different resources accessible, so the number of resources with unfamiliar vocabulary increases both absolutely and as a proportion of what is accessible. This is a recipe for less effective and less efficient searching. An important (though neglected) response to this problem is to provide search term recommender services. A simple form is a mapping from the familiar to the unfamiliar. In the subject index to first edition of the Dewey's decimal classification in 1876 is:

Railroads   385.

The sixth edition of Dewey's *Decimal Classification and Relativ Index for Libraries, Clippings, Notes, etc.* of 1899, used *railroad* to illustrate that the best link may vary according to the context ("in different connections"; Dewey 1899, 10), including:

Railroad	architecture	725
	corporations	385
	engineering	625
	law	385
	travel	614.863.

Since searchers come from different backgrounds, they do not have a single familiar vocabulary, so there should be a different set of subject indexing for each group of users. Until now that has not been economically feasible, but this can be approximated by creating multiple search term recommender services to any given vocabulary.

Imagine three doctors—an anesthesiologist, a drug therapy specialist, and a geriatrician—who each wanted recent literature on *cardiac arrest* (a medical term for a heart attack). "Cardiac arrest" itself is not a heading used in the standard Medical Subject Headings, or MeSH, vocabulary, so what would be the most effective MeSH headings to use? The three doctors are specialists. They do not have the same kind of interest in cardiac arrests. Each inhabits a different medical subculture. Each would not be interested in (and might not understand) the specialized literature of interest to the others. Suitably biased training sets can generate specialized search term recommendations for each.

From Citing to Linking

As our environment is increasingly a networked environment, the *citing* of authoritative resources in a print-on-paper environment gives way to *linking to* such resources. This has advantages. The online resource will have much more detailed information than a local authority list can. Consider place names. A local list can do little more than specify the preferred form of the name and as much detail as is needed to differentiate it from other places with the same name—typically, the type of place ("geographical feature type") and the geopolitical entity in which it is located. However, a place-name gazetteer will have all that and more, notably the latitude and longitude. Similarly with personal names, a local name authority list will have the preferred name, a note of other names also used, and just enough detail to differentiate it from other people encountered locally with the same name. A large, authoritative list, such as the name authority file of a national library or a biographical dictionary, will have a great deal of detail about the individual's life and career. The information is richer and can be drawn on as needed, for example, to make a map display or a time line.

Another benefit is that an invoked online resource can and should be continuously updated in a way that a printed volume cannot be, and the link makes this updating available whenever the link is invoked.

What, Who, Where, and When

So far we have discussed topics ("what") in general terms. There are, of course, different kinds of topic and some are different enough to justify specialized treatment. In the rest of this chapter, we show how three special cases (who, where, and when) are quite different and then how they are related.

Who: Personal Names

Personal names are important for authorship and biographical texts. The need to differentiate between different persons with the same name and aggregating different names for the same person is well understood in archives, libraries, museums, and elsewhere. However, the techniques for handling interpersonal relationships appears to have been rather neglected. Genealogists have experience with encoding family relationships (parent-child, spouse, etc.), but people can be related to each other in other important ways (e.g., teacher-pupil, business partner) for which techniques and terminology need further development.

Where: Geographical Areas, Place, and Space

Searching in a text environment is dominated by topical keywords or undifferentiated keywords, possibly including the names of persons, places, and institutions. However, for searching in some resources, such as socioeconomic data series and photographs, it becomes important to specify geographical location reliably and exactly. "Place" is a cultural construct, and this is reflected in place names, which, like topic names, are often multiple (e.g., Lisboa, Lisbon, Lisbona, Lisbonne, Lissabon); ambiguous (Galicia, Poland; Galicia, Spain); and unstable (e.g., St Petersburg became Leningrad then St Petersburg again).

Space, in contrast, is defined in physical terms of latitude and longitude, which provides descriptions that are neither ambiguous nor unstable. A large advantage of spatial coordinates is that they allow places to be shown on a map. There is, therefore, for geographical areas, a dual naming system of place and space: place names and spatial coordinates. A place-name gazetteer can be considered a kind of bilingual dictionary between places and spaces. A gazetteer enables place names to be disambiguated and places to be located on a map. A well-designed gazetteer will indicate when a place name was in use, thereby supporting changes over time.

When: Events and Time

Events and time tend to be mutually defining. Time is calibrated by physical events, and cultural epochs by cultural events. But physical events and cultural epochs are also calibrated by calendar time. In speech and in writing, we commonly mark time by reference to events, as in "after I graduated" or "before the Second World War." This duality of events and of time resembles the duality of place and space and invites a similar approach: the use of a directory relating named events to calendar time. Associating events with dates supports the construction of time lines and chronologies in the same way that a place-name gazetteer relates place names to spatial coordinates and map displays.

Relationships among Index Terms

So far we have spoken of indexes for topic, place, time, and persons as if the indexes for these facets were separate and independent, but in practice they are not, except in primitive examples. In a mature topical index such as the Library of Congress Subject Headings system, the topic heading will be commonly combined with geographical and chronological qualifiers, e.g., *Architecture—Japan—Meiji period, 1868–1912*. In other words, subject headings may have geographical and temporal components as well as topical.

A place-name gazetteer ordinarily indicates the kind of place (geographic "feature type") it is: castle, church, lake, city, etc. A physical feature is not the same as a topic, but any kind of feature can be treated as a topic. An individual castle is an instance of the category *castles*. Documents about castles generally may be helpful as well as any documents concerning this particular castle. And a discussion of the topic *castles* can be enriched by moving from the subject heading to the geographical feature type codes in the gazetteer in order to identify and to locate *instances* of castles in any region, so a mapping between feature types and subject headings can be useful. Since a well-designed gazetteer will also have an indication of *when* that name was in use, entries in gazetteers, like subject headings, can have temporal and topical as well as geographical aspects.

A time-period directory modeled on gazetteer designs would have a coding for kind of event or period. So, as with gazetteer entries, a specific event (e.g., an earthquake) can be linked to subject headings both by proper name (e.g., *Lisbon Earthquake 1755*) and also the literature on that class of events (e.g., *Earthquakes*). Events are specific to geographic areas, and so a proper time-period dictionary will have geographical codings, and it should be possible to link each event to both geographic subject headings and to gazetteer entries.

The texts of entries in biographical dictionaries are very rich in mentions of (1) kinds of activities, which could be linked to subject headings for that kind of activity; (2) places that could be linked to gazetteer entries and to geographic subject headings; (3) periods of time that could be linked to other, contemporaneous events via time-period directories, time lines, and chronologies; and (4) other people with whom the biographee interacted and for which biographical information could be found in biographical dictionaries and encyclopedias.

Although there are effective methods for handling peoples' names, methods for handling the events in their lives are much less developed. One approach is to categorize each biographical event or life activity as a four-aspect unit of what kind of activity (topical aspect), when (temporal aspect), where (geographical aspect), and with whom (biographical aspect). An attraction of this approach is that life events could be encoded with the terminology and methods already established, or being developed, for subject indexing, time periods, place names, and bio-graphical dictionaries.

Subject indexes, place-name gazetteers, time-period directories, and biographical dictionaries are quite different genres for quite different aspects of reality, but we find geographical connections, chronological links, and topical affinities across all four. There is a large and useful agenda in finding ways to build effective infrastructures of connections between these genres, because understanding requires a knowledge of context.

Facets and Context

We have discussed different kinds of topic using what, who, where, and when. The technical term for such differentiated categories is facets and the use of facets is central in classification and knowledge organization. Linked data, being normally a <sameAs> or similar relationship, are ordinarily mappings within a single facet. Likewise, in a library reference collection, the reference works are classified by facet-specific genres: biographies, geography (maps and place-name gazetteers), histories (and chronologies), and so on. But when we look beyond the heading in a catalog or a reference work and examine the content of the entry or beyond it in an explanation, we find no such limit to a single facet, but rather, multiple facets:

a library subject heading will have the main heading, but then commonly a geographic subdivision, chronological subdivision, and sometimes a personal name.

a place-name gazetteer will have a place name as a main heading, but then a geographical feature type and spatial markers for latitude and longitude. It could have a note of when that name was in use or the name of an especially significant associated person.

a time-period directory would have a period name as heading, qualified by what kind of period or event it was, time markers (calendar time), and where that period or event occurred.

a biographical dictionary will be arranged by personal name, followed by multiple instances of activity, date, other persons, and locations.

Actual instances will vary greatly, but the important point is that any main heading in a bibliography or catalog and any entry in any facet-limited reference work is likely to have qualifiers or explanations using any or all other facets. Figure 6 shows what one might expect, with lines connecting instances from different facets: time, place, who, and what. We see the same effect in complex precoordinate systems such as Library of Congress Subject Headings and the Universal Decimal Classification.

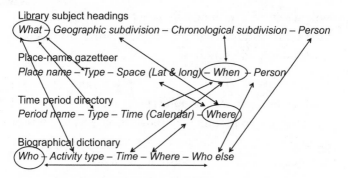

Figure 6   Entries in reference works divided by facet include other facets.

There may be reasons for the sequence of the facets in each row, but if, for the purposes of illustration, we disregard those reasons and we rearrange the elements in each row such that the facets align vertically, we get figure 7.

The realignment of the contents of each row in figure 6 to the arrangement by facet lines in figure 7 shows more clearly the potential for using vertical and horizontal links. For example, a library catalog subject heading "Lighthouses" could be linked to the geographical description code "Lthse" (Lighthouse) in a place-name gazetteer. The gazetteer would give locations of actual lighthouses, and the catalog would list publications about lighthouses. This combination provides far more information than either does separately by coupling the two quite different kinds of resource. As presented in figure 7, vertical mappings

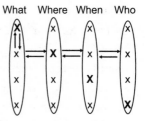

	What	Where	When	Who
WHAT (Library of Congress subject headings)	**X**	x	x	x
WHERE (Place name list)	x	**X**	x	x
WHEN (Time period dir.)	x	x	**X**	x
WHO (Biographical dict.)	x	x	x	**X**

Figure 7 Realignment by facet of the lines in figure 6, with examples of vertical and horizontal links.

provide links to additional vocabularies, which will lead to additional resources. Horizontal links provide additional context.

Summary

Document descriptions ("metadata") cover technical, administrative, and topical aspects and help us understand a document's character and whether it is of interest. Descriptions are created by assigning descriptive fragments, such as subject headings, to each document. Inverting this relationship—in effect, assigning documents to subject headings—creates indexes, thereby supporting a second purpose: discovery of documents of any given character. Problems arise from the differences between the many different languages, both natural and artificial (codes and classifications), in use. As a result, we need links that lead us from familiar terms to unfamiliar terms, especially in unfamiliar languages. In some cases, there are dual naming systems, such as place and space in geography, calendar and event in time, and formula and narrative explanation in mathematics, where the two aspects can be usefully combined. An important simplifying technique is the division in fundamentally different concepts (facets), such as who, what, when and where. Terms in each facet can be usefully linked across different languages, but these conceptually different elements are always combined together in real contexts, and there are many opportunities for taking advantage of these complex relationships.

This and the previous chapter examined how documents are described and how these descriptions can be organized and linked. In the next chapter, we look more closely at the mechanics of discovery and selection.

DISCOVERY AND SELECTION

Finding aids of many kinds exist to help the discovery, location, and selection of records and documents. A printed bibliography is a static structured interface for finding records describing documents. Here we examine more dynamic forms of selection aids: search engines; filtering systems; and retrieval systems, such as full-text search, library catalogs, web search, and enterprise search, for search within the resources of large organizations.

Search engines operate by identifying documents that have some specified characteristics. The basic mechanism is the matching of query and document. Retrieval systems match queries against a stable collection of documents, while filtering services use a stable query to select from a flow of documents. The term *information retrieval* was coined in 1950 and became widely adopted, but the earlier term *selection machine* provides a more accurate description of what is done.

Search practices vary by context and four different contexts will be considered: search of text files, a library catalog, web search, and search within the resources of an organization (enterprise search).

Retrieval and Selection

The word *retrieval* is ordinarily used to include quite different procedures: *identifying*, the discovery of documents, in the sense of establishing their existence; *locating* ("look-up"), when identified objects have known addresses; *fetching*, bringing an object from a known address; and *selecting*, in the sense of choosing. Locating and fetching are relatively straightforward procedures. It is the fourth, *selecting*, that is more interesting, especially when we do not know ahead of time what the choices are or even whether anything suitable is, in fact, available to be found, and so the challenge becomes to find a way to identify the *least unsuitable* documents.

These tasks can be divided into the following two situations:

1. locating and fetching known items using unambiguous requests, sometimes called data retrieval. This is

relatively straightforward, although the scale and complexity of the records can pose technical challenges.

2.   discovery and selection when the resources available are not precisely or unambiguously known, sometimes called document retrieval. Selection systems tend to be complex. They are usually proprietary, and their mechanisms opaque. All such systems have to be complete in order to work at all. These factors seem to have deflected attention from the simple nature of their components.

The core function of all finding and selecting systems is the matching of needs with documents and trying to separate (partition) those suitable for selection from the unsuitable. In mental selection, we think about different options and select one "within our head." On vacation we may decide to send postcards to some friends and relatives, but if we cannot remember their addresses confidently, we may need to look in a list of names and addresses, which we might also scan to see if we have forgotten someone who would want to receive a card. The need for selection aids becomes progressively more necessary as the size of a list or collection increases. Web search engines, searchable databases, library catalogs, and similar devices perform this function and have become everyday tools.

Selection machines are devices used to identify, locate, and fetch records. Because the choice is often so large and our familiarity with the options available inadequate, selection machines may also be used to choose for us. Web search engines, for example, select web pages for us. In nearly all cases, however, an initial shortlist selected by machine is followed by a human, mental selection from the choice provided by the machine.

In filtering systems, commonly used on incoming email, objects are represented, filtered (searched), and then selected for attention, relegated to other storage, or discarded. In this case the query, once developed, remains indefinitely in place as a stored instruction (selection rule) and is used to select incoming documents. Filters using stored queries on flows of data objects are symmetrical with retrieval systems with stably stored data objects and transient queries.

The Anatomy of Selection Machinery

General models of information retrieval systems are commonly found in information retrieval textbooks in the form shown in figure 8, with varying amounts of additional descriptive detail depending on the purpose of the description.

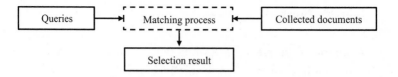

Figure 8 General model of selection systems.

There is a symmetry between queries and documents. Queries can be posed to a collection of documents ("ad hoc" search) or a flow of documents can be matched against a standing query (filtering).

There are many different procedures for matching queries with records: exact match; partial match; match using shortened words (truncation); positional and other relationships; logical combinations of query components (Boolean matching, e.g., *cats* AND *dogs*); and so on. There are limitless degrees of partial ("weaker") matching, and multiple techniques can be combined. Much of the very extensive technical literature on information retrieval is composed of descriptions of the use of minor variations. Description of the operation of any individual operational selection system is likely to require detailed diagrams of that particular system's components and workflow. Here, however, we are provide only a general description, and we start with a simple distinction between searching within a document and searching for a document.

Searching Text

A simple example of selection is the *Find* command provided in word processing software, which takes whatever the string of characters has been entered into the "find" field and then scans the entire text serially, word by word, comparing the query string with each word and then drawing attention to each match in the order found.

Where the amount of searchable text is large, the speed and efficiency of searching can be greatly improved by preprocessing the text to create an index that lists all words found in the text and provides the location within the text at which each word occurs. All words are indexed as found. In computing terms, this rearrangement of the elements is called an inverted file.

The traditional name for an index to the occurrences of words in a text is a *concordance*, but strictly speaking text searching uses strings of characters separated by spaces, not words. Words can have alternative spellings as well as ambiguous meanings, and quite different words with other meanings can have the same spelling; these variations are not distinguished. Uppercase and lower case letters will be treated as identical and punctuation marks excluded, but otherwise every sequence of characters is indexed automatically as found, regardless of meaning.

Full-text searching for character strings is very economical because the high cost of human indexing is avoided. It works well for discovery and selection to the extent that the query words used by the searcher match the terminology used in the texts being searched.

For efficiency, concordances may exclude ("stop") very frequently found words that are not expected to be useful when searching, such as articles (e.g., *a*, *an*, and *the*) and prepositions (e.g., *at*, *from*, and *to*). Many additional refinements can be provided by, for example, combining known variations in spelling and, where many different documents are being searched, the relative frequency of words in different documents can be used to give priority in the display of search results to documents containing the searched word more frequently.

More elaborate algorithms can be used to infer different meanings by looking at nearby words. For example, the character string *bank* is likely to refer to a river bank if used close to words such as *water, fish*, or *boat*, but is more likely to refer to a financial institution if close to words such as *finance*, *mortgage*, or *manager*. Another elaboration would be to represent more pairs of terms that commonly occur next to each other, such as *information* and *retrieval*, so that the significance of the combination can be represented. Much ingenuity has been invested in developing complex, algorithmically generated representations of combinations of words in a text.

A Library Catalog

A typical online library catalog provides a quite different approach. A carefully structured index—a database—is created. A precise and detailed description of each book or periodical in the library's collection is created in a carefully defined and standardized way as discussed in chapter 4, where an object-attribute-value approach was illustrated with the examples *person-age-45* and *book-topic-economics*.

In library catalogs, each aspect considered important—notably authorship, title, topic, date, size, publisher, and place of publication—is noted, using consistent terminology to create a precise representation of each one in a way that makes the catalog records compatible with records in other library catalogs worldwide. So, as an example of a set of attributes and values:

Author:	Wright, Alex.
Title:	*Glut : mastering information through the ages*.
Topic:	Information organization -- History.
Topic:	Information society -- History.
Call number:	Z666.5 .W75 2007
Date:	2007.

Size:	286 p.; 24 cm.
Publisher:	Joseph Henry Press
Place published:	Washington, D.C.

As noted in the previous chapter, descriptive metadata of this kind serves two different purposes: description and search. There are many other attributes that could be included, such as the binding, typeface, paper, and weight, that might be of interest for some library users, but catalogs and cataloging cost money, so investment is made only in the attributes considered most important. Further, since the creation and maintenance of searchable indexes consume significant resources, only some of the attributes are made searchable. In this example, often only the first four attributes (author, title, topic, and call number) would be searchable. The remaining four attributes (date, size, publisher, and place of publication) are usually not searchable but are displayed as description when a record has been found.

In early online catalogs, as with card catalogs, one specified an attribute and a value in the form FIND AUTHOR WRIGHT, ALEX. So to search by title one had to know the title exactly, or, at least, how it started: FIND TITLE GLUT would find all titles that started with the word "glut." As computing became more affordable, the technique of full-text search described above was added to allow search for individual words within titles. In addition, support became available for compound queries, so-called Boolean searches, in the form FIND TITLE GLUT AND AUTHOR WRIGHT, ALEX, where only records that satisfied both conditions would be retrieved, or FIND TITLE GLUT OR AUTHOR WRIGHT, ALEX, where records satisfying either condition would be retrieved.

The choice of attributes and the presentation of values follows long-established cataloging codes designed to achieve consistency and interoperability. The creation of the records, the preparation of searchable indexes, the procedure for posing queries, and the display of search results involves a series of steps. Analysis of these steps shows a chain of records and operations alternating. The books are subjected to a cataloging process resulting in catalog records; the catalog records are operated upon to generate the searchable index; the user's query is formalized to become a formal query; formal query and the searchable index are matched to yield the selected set, the selected set is sorted and processed for display, and so on. Each process derives a new set. These processes are of two quite different types: those that modify the objects being processed, and those that rearrange the objects. These two processes correspond to Fairthorne's marking and parking, noted in chapter 4.

In practice, searching is commonly a series of selection stages. One might start by browsing subject headings (a first search) and when a suitable subject heading has been selected, search for documents associated with that subject heading (a second search) to find one or more selected documents, which when inspected suggest that a modified search (a third search) would be more useful, and so on.

Appendix A provides a more detailed explanation of this precisely designed system, with its carefully edited records.

Searching the Web

The carefully prepared records, standardized formats, and precise search options found in library catalogs and in searchable, well-edited databases were developed before the emergence of the World Wide Web. The web posed a new challenge because web pages do not have the standardized, carefully edited, and well-structured content that characterizes library catalog records. Subject description is commonly lacking or, if provided, not standardized. The creators of web pages and other documents may also add description that may be intentionally misleading in order to attract attention. The lack of control over the creation of web pages and the sheer number of them make it impossible to catalog the web in any way comparable to library cataloging.

The basic solution adopted is simple. The web is downloaded and treated as text. Software designed to crawl around the web downloads as many pages as possible. Each page found by a web-crawler is copied and stored. Each word in each stored page is used to produce an index to that page. All the index entries to all the pages are combined to form a unified index to all of the pages collected. Every query is expressed in the form of one or more words and leads through the unified index to web pages containing one or more of those words.

This approach allows extremely economical and rapid selection from vast numbers of web pages, but because of size of the web, the result of any query is likely to be inconveniently large and in no useful order. In addition to knowing which documents are "on topic," it would be helpful to know which ones are in some sense preferable to others and to give those priority in the presentation of the search results. The solution was to adapt a principle from academic scholarship. Since writings considered significant are more likely to be cited than those that are not, the frequency of citations to any given book or article can be considered an indicator of importance or, at least, of popularity. Web pages cite each other with links, so a count of the links to any given web page can be used in the same way to sort and to rank the pages found in a web search. This combination of downloading, index building, and page ranking provides a powerful and efficient selection service,

The lack of control over the creation of web pages and the sheer number of them make it impossible to catalog the web in any way comparable to library cataloging.

even though major simplifications (reliance on character strings and page ranking) are made.

The enormous demand for web searching allows for substantial revenue from advertisements inserted into the displayed results and from payments for more prominent display of sponsored pages. Although this revenue would be insufficient for the conventional cataloging of every web page, it does allow the development of very sophisticated software to improve the search results. Spell-checking software and other techniques used for full-text search can be used to suggest alternative search results. Dictionaries and thesauri can be used to elaborate the searchable index with some vocabulary control (e.g., connecting synonyms and variant spellings). When recorded, the history of an individual's previous searches can analyzed to infer the searcher's intention, to suggest related options, and to display advertisements likely to be of interest.

Other Examples

Large organizations in both public and private sectors need control over their corporate records and depend on the ability to find the right material when needed ("enterprise search"). The scale, while far less than the web, can be large. More importantly, over time, changes in

This combination of downloading, index building, and page ranking provides a powerful and efficient selection service, even though major simplifications (reliance on character strings and page ranking) are made.

standards, terminology, and software lead to both records and software becoming obsolescent and so maintaining access, security, and preservation becomes increasingly difficult. Mergers and takeovers result in the need to cope with alien material and previously unsupported software. In this difficult environment, different approaches will be combined. As in library catalogs, controlled vocabularies, often called *thesauri* or *ontologies*, will be used where affordable along with the techniques used in full-text search. Document management software may be used to provide a more or less coherent environment for all or most of the corporate records.

In searching text, one can look for words that tend to occur together. Similarly, data sets of any kind can be examined to look for statistically significant relationships that might suggest unknown, unexpected, or interesting relationships and anomalies. The "data mining" of sales records, of social media, and of news reports are examples.

Summary

The phrase *information retrieval* is used for finding and fetching already known documents, as well the more difficult task of search and discovery of previously unknown resources. The basic approach is to match queries against documents or their descriptions. Texts can be searched serially, but it is more efficient to use the words in the text to make an index. Alternatively, as in the case of library catalogs, a database of carefully prepared descriptions can be searched. All selection machinery, both filtering services and retrieval systems, can be seen to be composed of just two types of component: objects (data sets) and operations on them. There are only two kinds of operations: *transforming*, or deriving modified versions or representations of objects, and *arranging* (or rearranging) objects by combining, dividing, ranking, and other comparable sorting operations. These two operations are Fairthorne's *marking* and *parking*, and they can be described as semantic and syntactic, respectively. More familiar terms would be *description* and *arrangement*.

In the next chapter, we will examine how selection methods are evaluated.

EVALUATION OF
SELECTION METHODS

When serious studies of retrieval evaluation started in the 1960s, relevance was adopted as the criterion of selection success and measured in two ways: completeness in selecting relevant documents (recall) and the quality in terms of selecting only relevant documents (precision). In practice, a trade-off was found. Achieving a more complete selection of relevant documents tended to also increase the number of nonrelevant documents, while seeking to reduce the number of nonrelevant documents selected tended to reduce the completeness of the selection of relevant ones.

Relevance is a central concept in information retrieval and dominates the evaluation of selection systems, but there are problems with it. In practice, treating documents as simply relevant or nonrelevant is a very convenient but unrealistic simplification. Documents are often somewhat

In practice, treating documents as simply relevant or nonrelevant is a very convenient but unrealistic simplification.

relevant; or their relevance is situational depending on what documents have already been selected; or they are relevant to one person but not to another, or at one time but not at another. The explanation lies in the evidential nature of documents and the cognitive needs relative to that evidential role.

Relevance, Recall, and Precision

1. *Recall* is a measure of completeness. For any given query, how completely were relevant documents retrieved? Were all the relevant documents retrieved? If not, how many? What proportion? The answer is usually expressed as the percentage of the relevant documents in a collection that were found by the retrieval system in response to a query. So, for example, if there were 10 relevant documents in the collection but only eight of them were retrieved, the recall performance was eight out of 10, or 80%. The results for multiple different queries could be averaged to provide a more broad-based assessment.

2. *Precision* is a measure of purity. Did the retrieved set include only relevant documents, or were some unwanted, nonrelevant documents ("false drops") also retrieved in error? Precision is used as a technical term for the proportion of the documents in a retrieved set that is relevant to

the query. If 10 documents were retrieved but only six were relevant and four were not, then precision was six out of 10, or 60%.

The obvious objective of retrieving all of the relevant items (perfect recall) and only relevant items (perfect precision) is rarely achieved in practice. Efforts to increase completeness in retrieval performance (higher recall) tend to increase the number of nonrelevant documents also retrieved (lower precision). Efforts to avoid nonrelevant items in order to achieve high precision tend also to increase the number of relevant items that are not retrieved (lower recall). One may want selection systems that would retrieve all and only relevant documents, but in practice it seems that one has to choose between seeking all but not only relevant items or only but not all relevant items. Either way, the results are less than perfect. These empirical results happen often enough to be accepted as normal. Appendix B explains why this happens.

Recall with Random, Perfect, and Realistic Retrieval

If documents are retrieved at random from a collection, the odds are always the same that the next document retrieved will be relevant. Suppose, for example, that a hundred documents in a collection of a thousand documents (just 10%) are relevant to a given query. Then, if documents are retrieved from the collection at random, the odds of the next document retrieved being relevant would remain, in this example, 100 in 1,000, which is 10 in 100, or 10%. As a result, the number of relevant documents retrieved would grow slowly and would not be completed (100% recall) until all or almost all of the documents in the collection had been retrieved.

A perfect retrieval system would retrieve only relevant documents until no more were left. In this ideal case, the recall measure would increase rapidly to 100% when the first 100 documents (all relevant) had been retrieved. Of course, any additional documents retrieved beyond the first hundred would necessarily have to be nonrelevant. But since all the relevant documents have been retrieved by then, the recall measure remains perfect at 100%.

It is realistic to assume that any actual retrieval system will be less than perfect but better than retrieval at random, so performance will be somewhere between those two theoretical extremes. What happens is that since retrieval is better than random, there is early success: the first documents will tend to be relevant ones, and so the recall performance will initially rise quickly as retrieval proceeds. But a consequence of this early success is that the proportion of relevant documents in the pool of not-yet-retrieved documents steadily decreases. As a result, although a realistic retrieval starts well, improvement gradually slows as the proportion of still-retrievable relevant documents in the collection diminishes. Achieving retrieval of every last relevant document (100% recall) might not be achieved until most or even all of the documents in the collection have been retrieved.

Precision with Random, Perfect, and Realistic Retrieval

Similarly, if documents are retrieved at random, the odds are always the same—only one in 10 in our example—that the next document retrieved will be relevant, so precision will tend to be around 10%, however many documents are retrieved.

With perfect retrieval, however, the first 100 documents retrieved will all be relevant, and so precision will start and remain at 100%. Of course, any additional documents retrieved beyond that first hundred would necessarily have to be nonrelevant, and thus, if retrieval is continued, precision will gradually decline to the limit of 10% if all the documents in the collection are retrieved.

With any actual retrieval system, being less than perfect but better than random, since retrieval is better than random, there is early success, and the first documents will tend to be relevant ones. As a result, precision will start high, but then gradually decline if retrieval continues and the proportion of relevant documents among those retrieved diminishes.

Trade-off between Recall and Precision

Ideally one would retrieve *all* relevant documents (perfect recall) and retrieve *only* relevant documents (perfect precision), and to the extent that recall and precision are not perfect, both should be improved. However, experience shows that in practice there is a trade-off. Wider searching to retrieve more relevant documents will tend to result in retrieving more nonrelevant documents, too, so improved recall tends to be at the expense of precision. Meanwhile, more careful retrieval intended to exclude nonrelevant documents from retrieval (improved precision) will also tend to yield less complete retrieval, so improved precision tends to be at the expense of recall. One has a choice of emphasizing *all-but-not-only* or *only-but-not-all*, but not both at the same time. (For a more detailed explanation, see Appendix B.)

Some Problems with Relevance

Relevance is the traditional criterion in the evaluation of selection systems and is widely considered to be the most central concept in the field. But relevance is deeply problematic in several ways, including its definition. "Relevant" could be those items wanted by the inquirer, those that will please, or those that are most useful. However, *want*, *please*, and *useful* are not the same. Further, assessments will be highly subjective and, since the search is presumed to be by someone inadequately informed, are likely to be unreliable.

Relevance is highly situational, depending on what the inquirer already knows. And relevance is unstable because the inquirer is, or should be, actively learning, so the very fact of retrieving informative documents should change the relevance status of documents for the searcher.

The standard assumption that all items are independent in the sense that the relevance of one item does not affect the relevance of any other item is a convenient but unconvincing simplification. If two documents are very similar, one usually does not need both. Further, the relative relevance of documents is unstable because the population of documents is always changing.

The discussion above also assumes that relevance is binary: either a document is relevant, or it is not. This, too, is unrealistic. In practice, documents are more likely to be somewhat relevant, partially relevant, marginally relevant, or of uncertain relevance. Added to all this, judgments concerning relevance tend to be inconsistent between different judges and also over time for the same judge.

Information services are purposive, and a document is said to be relevant if it serves someone's mental activity beneficially. This raises further difficulties: whose benefit? Who determines what is beneficial? How is the benefit to be measured?

Why Relevance Is Difficult

With all these difficulties, it is not surprising that, although relevance has been regarded as central to information science, it remains problematic despite sustained attention by many talented minds. Howard White (2010) provides an excellent account of relevance theory. He states, correctly, that although relevance is well understood, it resists satisfying definition, observation, or scientific treatment, as has been noted by critics all along.

To be relevant, a document must be useful to an actual human being's mental activity. Therefore, relevance is subjective, idiosyncratic, hard to predict, and unstable. (Relevance to a specific need of a specific person is sometimes named pertinence.) Ordinarily, one can only make a judicious guess that a given document is likely to be relevant to a given query for a supposed population of users at some point in time.

To be relevant, a document must be useful to an actual human being's mental activity. Therefore, relevance is subjective, idiosyncratic, hard to predict, and unstable.

The basic problem is that documents have both physical and mental aspects. Scientific measurement depends on there being something physical to measure. The physical aspects of documents can be measured and so treated scientifically, but the highly situational, unstable, idiosyncratic, and subjective mental angle cannot. Thus, because every document also has a significant but inaccessible mental aspect, its relevance cannot be measured scientifically. For this reason, relevance can never be satisfactorily a scientific matter in the normative sense of formal and physical sciences such as mathematics and physics, based on formal conjecture and refutation.

In practice, we fall back on distant substitutes. We can use the physical angle only, primarily of coded character strings, and use character strings in a query to discover similar character strings in documents that might be discourse on the same topic. The matching of character strings works quite well, but not very reliably. We can ask a jury to predict whether a document is likely to be relevant to a hypothetical inquirer. We can ask an inquirer, after a search, whether a document was relevant, but either judgment might not be valid for someone else or for the same person at another time.

A scientific approach to relevance could work very well if a document had only a physical aspect and not also a mental one. We see this situation in the case of the modeling of signaling reliability developed by Claude Shannon as communication theory and now better known as information theory. The scientific quality and practical utility of this model is beyond question, and it can be achieved because no mental or social properties are involved, only physical properties. A desire to make this information theory a central component in library and information science has not proven successful, and the reason is not hard to see. For any information science concerned with what individuals know requires a mental angle, and Shannon-Weaver information theory is powerful precisely because it excludes the mental angle. It can be useful as a tool, just as queuing theory and other quantitative tools can be, but despite its name it cannot claim any greater special status.

Ultimately, then, relevance is a convenient conjectured relationship, and it is not surprising that despite 50 years of hard work by talented researchers, it remains ill-defined and not measurable in any direct way. Nevertheless, such a measure is needed, so convenient substitutes, usually the use of similar words, are used instead: if someone asks for documents about bicycles, then one infers that any document including the word "bicycle" is likely to be, at least in part, about bicycles and so worth adding to the set of selected documents.

Summary

Relevance is the most central concept in the evaluation of selection systems, but its use as a measure depends on very severe simplification of a complex reality. There is necessarily a trade-off between the completeness of selection (recall) and the purity of selection (precision). A more fundamental problem is that status as a document involves more than physical existence. There is a cognitive element as well which resists measurement and, as a result, treating relevance quantitatively can be very useful, yet unscientific.

SUMMARY AND REFLECTIONS

Summary

The word *information* commonly refers to physical stuff such as bits, books, and other physical media, any physical thing perceived as signifying something: documents, in a broad sense. It is easy to think of information as stuff, but the example of a passport reveals how deeply embedded in social activity that stuff can be.

The growing importance of information derives from the progressive division of labor, which enabled our transition from hunters and gatherers to an increasingly complex society. We depend more and more on cooperation, which means, in practice, dependence on information. This increased dependence is not neutral, because it is used purposefully to advance the many agendas of everyone involved, acting alone, in groups, or through organizations. Strictly speaking, all associations, all societies, depend on collaboration and communication. What is meant by an *information society* is that the way we live has become increasingly characterized by the use of documents in many forms. Specialized, technical uses of the word "information" that are unrelated to human knowing are outside our present interests.

All living creatures depend for survival on their ability to sense, to make sense, and to react appropriately. Accordingly, communication, providing some expression for others to respond to, is crucial for any collaboration. Humans are different in their exceptional ability in the use of language, the making of images, the display of objects, and the use of tools. Since prehistoric times, four kinds of information technology have become increasingly important: writing, printing, telecommunication, and copying, each fueled by successive engineering advances, including steam, electricity, photography, and, now, digital computing.

The rising tide of documents brought initiatives to organize them, the challenge of knowing what to trust, and imaginative metaphorical language to describe both problems and opportunities.

Ordinarily, documents are graphic records, usually text, created to express some meaning. However, almost anything can be made to serve as a document, such as a leek to express Welsh identity. On a semiotic view,

What is meant by an *information society* is that the way we live has become increasingly characterized by the use of documents in many forms.

meaning is constructed in the mind of the viewer, so any object might be perceived as signifying something and, in that sense, could be considered a document. So if we hold to the idea of documents being evidence, a wide variety of objects and actions could be regarded as being "documents" in this extended sense. Anything regarded as a document must, in addition to having a physical form, be perceived as signifying something and depend on shared understandings ("cultural codes"). Data sets are a type of document, but the infrastructure making digital data sets accessible for use over time is much less developed than for printed material. The requirements are in principle the same. Scholarly practices, infrastructure, and the field known variously as bibliography, documentation, or information science needs modernizing accordingly.

Individuals use documents in varied ways: to learn, to verify, to communicate, to record, to enjoy, and to monitor. Increasingly, our interaction with others is through messages and other documents. How we use them and what we understand from them are integral parts of our culture. We each live in small but complex worlds, and our writing, reading, and understanding all occur within cultural contexts. Even facts need to be understood in context.

The problem of discovering documents we need and of obtaining a copy when needed is handled by making descriptions and forming collections, or marking and parking. Lists are virtual collections. Search depends on assigning descriptions to documents and then matching queries to the descriptions, but describing and querying can be difficult because we draw on the language of the past and on assumptions about the future.

Naming the topics of documents varies by notation (words or codes), vocabulary control (standardized terminology), combinations for complex topics (e.g., venetian blind, blind Venetian), and fineness (how detailed). Describing is a language activity and, since language evolves, descriptions are obsolescent. Because language is cultural, descriptions of sensitive topics may well be contested.

Document descriptions ("metadata") cover technical, administrative, and topical aspects and help us understand a document's character and whether or not it is of interest. Descriptions are created by associating descriptive fragments, such as subject headings, with each document. Inverting this relationship, associating documents with subject headings, creates indexes, thereby supporting a second purpose: discovery of documents of any given character. Problems arise from the differences between the many different languages, both natural and artificial (codes and classifications) in use. As a result, we need links that guide us from familiar terms in a familiar language to unfamiliar terms in unfamiliar languages. In some cases, there are dual naming systems, such as place and space in geography, calendar and event in time, and formula and narrative explanation in mathematics, where the two modes can be usefully combined. An important simplifying technique is division into fundamentally different types of concepts (*facets*) such as who, what, when, and where. Terms of each type can be usefully linked across different languages, but these conceptually different elements are always combined together in real contexts, and there are many opportunities for taking advantage of these complex relationships.

All selection machinery—for search, discovery, filtering, and retrieval systems—can be viewed as being composed of combinations of just two primitive types: objects (data) and operations on them. There are just two kinds of operations: transforming (deriving modified versions or representations of objects) and arranging or rearranging objects (combining, dividing, sorting, ranking). These two operations, marking and parking, can be described as semantic and syntactic, respectively. More familiar terms would be description and arrangement. Selection systems can be seen as a sequence of one or the other of these two types of operation: the derivation of a modified set of objects or the creation of a different arrangement of them.

The traditional criterion in the evaluation of selection systems is *relevance*, a very central concept in the field. The idea is that all and only relevant items should be selected, but this simple wish is deeply problematic in several ways. *Relevant* could be those items wanted or needed by the inquirer, or those that will please or be most useful. However, *want*, *need*, *please*, and *useful* are not the same, and assessments will be highly subjective. Since a search is presumed to be by someone inadequately informed, assessment is likely to be unreliable. Relevance is highly situational, depending on what the inquirer already knows, and unstable because the inquirer is, or should be, actively learning. Further, the goals of *all* and *only* relevant are in conflict, because in practice one can seek to emphasize *all* (recall) only at the expense of *only* (precision) and vice versa. Relevance is problematic because documents are not merely physical. Objects are considered documents because they are regarded as evidence of some kind, and it is this subjective aspect that undermines objective, quantitative measurement.

After this summary, we can add some reflections.

The Past and the Future

In the first chapter, my passport was used to introduce the role of technology, and in chapter 2, we noted how, after prehistoric times, humans moved beyond speech, dance, gesture, and, drawing with new lines of technical development: writing, printing, telecommunications, and copying. New tools (steam, electricity, photography, and, now, digital computing) enabled an explosion of communications, records, and documents of many kinds, leading to the rise of an addition line of technical development for finding and selecting the few that are wanted at any point in time from the ever-growing flood. Much of information technology can be seen as a sustained effort to diminish the effects of separation in space and time. We can extrapolate the past and present into the future using the same components and assuming continuing improvements in technology:

1. *writing*, a means for recording speech, is moving steadily toward the *recording of everything*.

2. *printing*, the multiplication of texts, is evolving into the *reproducing of anything*.

3. *telecommunications*, in effect the transportation of documents, becomes, with sustained improvement, effectively *pervasive simultaneous interaction*.

4. *document copying*, because it depends technically on the use of image analysis and enhancement, leads to more than just the making of additional copies. The logical development of document copying is *document analysis and representation*, including visualization and the analysis of data sets.

Much of information
technology can be seen
as a sustained effort
to diminish the effects
of separation in space
and time.

5. *finding and selecting* moves steadily toward connecting and relating every record with every other record in an all-embracing web.

All of the above depends on infrastructure, including legal regimes underlying commerce and intellectual property, standardized terminology in metadata, markets, subsidies, and restrictions relating to decency, privacy, security, and other cultural values. So the opportunities for mental engagement with (physical) documents is heavily framed by social forces, with both commercial and governmental organizations strongly motivated to monitor and record what we do.

With the general adoption of digital technology, the kind of technology combination seen in the coupling of photography and printing to create photolithography extends across all varieties of technical development, leading to an environment in which different genres can be woven together into a new and richer tapestry. Projecting these technologies forward, then, leads to a society characterized by ubiquitous recording, pervasive reproduction, simultaneous interaction regardless of geographical distance, more powerful analysis of records, and an absence of privacy. Increasingly, there is a shift from individuals deriving benefits from the use of documents to documentary regimes seeking to influence, control, and benefit from individuals.

Coping: Orality, Literacy, and Documentality

If we accept that these or any similar future projections are valid, when we look backward from an imaged future back into the historical past, what do they imply about how we cope with these developments?

The first case, in which writing extends toward the recording of anything, is of interest because much has been made of the fixity of writing and how it differs from oral discussion. At a time when orality was dominant, and rhetoric, the art of discourse, was central to education, Socrates famously observed in Plato's *Phaedrus* that writing was inferior to discussion because writing is inanimate. Writing cannot explain itself or answer questions or correct itself as circumstances change. However, the fixity of writing has also been seen as momentous in providing continuity and consistency across time and space and, thereby, enabling larger and more standardized forms of social organization.

Much has been made of the transition from an oral to a literate culture and, how, for example, with the ability to record what we need to remember, mental memory techniques (mnemonics) are used less. This is a simplification. First, the emphasis on orality disregards the important communicative roles of dance, music, and ritual. Second, the effect was additive. Literacy was added to and affected orality, just as digital techniques are affecting writing and speech.

Increasingly, there is a shift from individuals deriving benefits from the use of documents to documentary regimes seeking to influence, control, and benefit from individuals.

There is more to documents than literacy, because the records that affect us are decreasingly read or acted upon by humans, at least not directly. Commerce and transportation, for example, now depend on communication using printed bar codes. We see them and we know what they are, but we are not able by ourselves to read or interpret them. In the emerging digital environment of bar codes, sensors, and databases, the documents that shape our lives are decreasingly readable by humans. They are decreasingly visible to the human eye.

Although people do and must increasingly use documents, in the last resort they ultimately fall back on asking for guidance from friends they trust, suggesting that is the more basic, primal action. Examples of censorship and resistance to writings can also be seen in this frame if we view, for example, Nazi book burnings as part of the Nazi desire to protect and strengthen culture, as they understood it, from the advance of modernist civilization.

Documents are increasingly machine readable for many different reasons. Electronic, machine-readable records are not humanly legible. Some kind of special rendering or visualization is necessary even for plain text. Machines are programmed to operate on them. In fact we delegate the reading of digital documents to digital technologies. We "read" them vicariously. Mostly, machines operate on them and use our instructions to derive new records from them on a vast scale that we cannot ordinarily follow. This is no longer "literacy" in any meaningful sense, but a new phase of communicating and commemorating, and some new term is needed. We might reasonably refer to a transition from a literate society to a document society, and, if we do, we should remember that the process is additive. Our document society also includes literacy and orality (and dance and drawing and other performances).

What Kind of a Field?

What kind of a field is the study of information? It should by now be clear that discourse in this field is full of figurative and conjectural language: *world brain*, *external memory*, *relevance*, *work* (as an imputed set of ideas), *content*, *meme*, *community knowledge*, *information society*, and so on. Only a living creature can know, but it is convenient to refer to documents as recorded knowledge and to machinery or an institution as knowing. This imaginative language has a useful role and is typical of changing fields, but there is also a need for it to be complemented by careful, rigorous analysis if we are to have a clear understanding of information and society.

The study of information is also conjectural. Common examples of conjecture are the use of *relevance*, the conjectured suitability of a document for some cognitive purpose, and *work*, when used abstractly for a body of intellectual or artistic achievement distinct from the physical expressions and manifestations of that achievement.

Since all manifestations of information are invariably physical, and all information systems and services are humanly made, information science is an example of what Herb Simon called the sciences of the artificial. At the same time, information, when in relation to society, is essentially cultural. The desire to be more scientific, meaning more formal and more quantitative, is often sought by excluding cultural aspects that resist formal definitions, precise measurement, and logical operations. Formal approaches to "information" are well developed and very useful for many practical purposes. Nevertheless, the restrictive foundation ensures a limited scope. In contrast, we have preferred a more realistic approach by insisting that the study of information be rooted in the process of informing, of becoming informed, of human knowing. Both approaches are valid. They are, however, different.

There is a tension between formal systems of great practical use and the knowledge that these helpful devices depend on making simplifying assumptions that do not in fact fully reflect reality. Such compromise is also true of other fields that deal with human behavior. Economics is an example: the virtuoso methods of microeconomic analysis are very powerful, but they assume a degree of rationality not characteristic of human behavior. Similar tension can be found in linguistics and other social and humanities fields. In a way, this is reassuring because it makes information science emerge as comparable to other well-developed fields of study.

It will be clear from the passport example with which we began and from all that has followed that only an approach that combines the physical, the mental, and the social aspects can be adequate for the challenge of examining the complex relationships of information and society.

APPENDIX A:
ANATOMY OF SELECTION

In chapter 7, we noted that the basic structure of information retrieval is usually shown in textbooks in the form shown in figure 9, with varying amounts of additional descriptive detail depending on the purpose of the description. There is a symmetry between queries and documents.

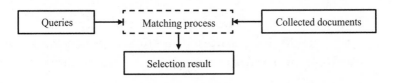

Figure 9   General model of selection systems.

A typical online library catalog uses a highly structured database, and we use a generalized description to illustrate how such a system works.

In the broader environment, there are the documents to be cataloged; humans who have queries; and a variety of external resources, such as the standardized vocabularies (e.g., the U.S. Library of Congress Subject Headings), the subject classification scheme being used, sources of catalog records, and the rules and procedures to be followed.

The output is the search result—the retrieved set—although there will also be feedback reports, such as error messages.

What happens inside the system is shown in figure 10.

Figure 10 illustrates a model of a library catalog. Solid boxes contain processes. Dashed boxes contain records, either queries or catalog records. Italics show optional components, and arrows indicate flows. The documents to be cataloged are shown at top right (box 1). A cataloging process (box 2) may draw on cataloging rules, standard vocabularies, and catalog copy from elsewhere (box 3) and result in a set of catalog records (box 4). In practice, not all parts of catalog records are searchable, so a further process determines the choice of access points (box 5), yielding the searchable set of index entries, also known as the entry vocabulary (box 6).

Library users have their queries (box 7) and the expression of these queries needs to be adapted to the terminology of retrieval system (box 8) to select one or more acceptable search terms (box 9), which can then be formulated (box 10) into a formal query (box 11) for matching (box 12) against searchable terms—"entry vocabulary" (box 6)—to derive a search result or "retrieved set" (box 13). Usually, the initially retrieved set is sorted (box 14) for display of the search result (box 15).

Some features of figure 10 invite attention.

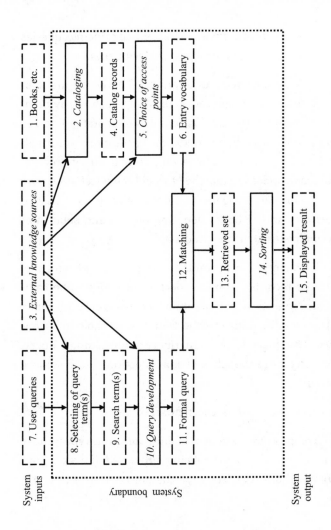

Figure 10 A minimally complete model of a library catalog.

1.   The structure is symmetrical and, in principle, queries are logically interchangeable with documents.

2.   *Objects* and *processes* alternate. The books are subjected to a cataloging process resulting in the deriving of catalog records; the catalog records are operated upon to generate the searchable index; the user's query is formalized to become a formal query; formal query and the searchable index are matched to yield the selected set; and so on. This pattern is marked graphically by using dashed lines around the boxes denoting objects and solid lines around boxes denoting processes.

3.   Each object box contains a collection (set) of zero, one, or more records: From a collection of books to be cataloged, a collection (set) of catalog records is derived, which is then modified into a collection of searchable index entries. The query flow ordinarily contains a single query. The outcome of the selection is a collection of zero or more records.

4.   Each process derives a new set.

5.   The processes are of two quite different types: those that *modify* the objects being processed (boxes 2 and 10) and those that *rearrange* the objects (boxes 5, 8, 12, and 14).

6.   In practice, searching is commonly a series of multiple selection stages. For example, one might start by browsing subject headings (a first search); when a suitable subject heading has been selected, search for documents associated with that subject heading (a second search); and then find that one or more selected documents suggest that a modified search (a third search) would be worthwhile; and so on.

APPENDIX B: RETRIEVAL
EVALUATION MEASURES

As explained in chapter 8, relevance is the standard measure for the evaluation of selection systems. It is used as a binary measure: documents are judged to be either relevant or not relevant to a given query. Given a set of relevance judgments, performance is assessed in two ways: *recall* is the completeness of selection performance, measured as the proportion of the relevant documents that were successfully selected; and *precision* is ability of the selection system to select relevant documents and not nonrelevant documents, measured as the proportion of the selected documents that are relevant. Here we use graphs to show these two measures and the relationship between them given different selection performances.

Recall Graphed

We assume a collection of 1,000 documents, of which 100 are relevant to a query. These numbers may be unrealistic, but they are convenient for explanation.

A graph (figure 11) is calibrated 0–1,000 on the horizontal axis for the number of documents in the collection selected (the retrieved set) and vertically 0–100% for recall, the proportion of the relevant 100 documents that have been retrieved. A recall graph necessarily starts at the origin (bottom left, O) when no items have been retrieved and must end when all documents, relevant or not, have been retrieved at the top right corner (A). So all recall curves must start at the origin, lower left, and end at the top right. The interest is in the shape of the line from O to A.

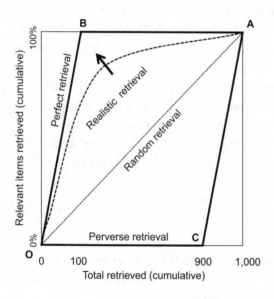

Figure 11 Recall graph for random retrieval, perfect retrieval, realistic retrieval, and perverse retrieval.

Figure 11 shows recall with lines from O to A for random retrieval (dotted line), perfect retrieval (thick line, OBA), realistic retrieval (dashed curve), and perverse retrieval (lower thick line, OCA).

If documents were retrieved at random, the odds are always the same that the next document retrieved will be relevant (in this example, 1 in 10), so the recall curve would be a diagonal straight line from the origin (O) and ending in the top right corner (A), shown here as a dotted line.

A perfect retrieval system would retrieve only relevant items until no more were left, and if one continued to retrieve, any further retrievable documents would necessarily have to be nonrelevant. This perfect selection performance is plotted in figure 11 as a steeply rising line from the origin (O) to the top (at B) which is reached, in our example, when all 100% of the 100 relevant items have been retrieved. Further retrieval could only be of the remaining items (all nonrelevant), so the line would turn right and move horizontally along the top margin to the top right-hand corner from B to A.

It is realistic to assume that any actual retrieval system will be less than perfect but better than retrieval at random, and so the performance curve will be somewhere between the lines for perfect and for random. What happens is that the ratio of relevant items retrieved to nonrelevant items retrieved is better than random, and so the realistic line rises more steeply than the random line. But a consequence of this early success is that the pool of not-yet-retrieved relevant items decreases more rapidly than with random retrieval. As a result, although a realistic retrieval curve must rise faster at first than the straight diagonal line for random retrieval, it must gradually flatten out until it reaches the top right-hand corner (A) where all recall curves must end. Since no operational system is exactly and always perfect, the curve must also run below the line for perfect retrieval, and so it must always be within the triangle OBC and is likely to be more or less like the curved dashed line drawn. The better the performance of a retrieval system, the closer its recall curve will be closer to the perfect retrieval line than to the random retrieval line, tending in the direction of the arrow.

For theoretical completeness we can also draw the recall curve for a perfectly awful retrieval system that insisted on retrieving all and only nonrelevant items until no more were left and thereafter could only retrieve relevant items. We call this imagined case perverse retrieval and a perverse retrieval curve would run straight horizontally from O to C, then necessarily rising to A.

In conclusion,

1. the parallelogram OBAC defines all possible recall performances.

2.   only systems achieving better than random retrieval will be of any practical interest, so all realistic systems will have recall curves within the triangle OBA.

3.   the better the retrieval performance, the closer the actual recall curve will be to the perfect retrieval curve (OBA) and away from the diagonal random retrieval recall curve (OA). Differently stated, the better the retrieval performance, the more its curve will move in the direction of the arrow.

Precision Graphed

A comparable graph can be drawn for precision. See figure 12.

In our example, 100 out of the 1,000 items in the collection are relevant, so documents retrieved at random will tend to be composed of one relevant item for every nine nonrelevant. Precision is expressed as a percent, so random retrieval has a precision of 10% regardless of how many items are retrieved. This is shown by the horizontal dotted line from D to E.

A perfect retrieval system would initially yield only relevant items, so it starts and remains at 100% precision until all the 100 relevant items have been retrieved (at point B). After that, only nonrelevant items remain, so the

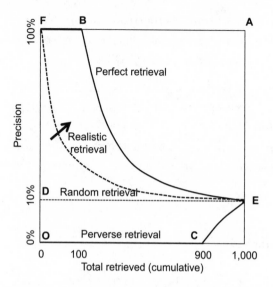

Figure 12 Precision graph showing lines for random retrieval, perfect retrieval, perverse retrieval, and realistic retrieval.

retrieved set becomes progressively more diluted with nonrelevant items until, when the entire collection has been retrieved, precision reflects the collection as a whole. The perfect retrieval curve changes direction at point B and follows a concave curve down to point E.

Correspondingly, a perverse retrieval system initially retrieves all and only nonrelevant items, so until all the 900 nonrelevant items have been retrieved precision remains at zero and the line is horizontal from O to C. Then all remaining documents are relevant so precision can only increase, as shown by the convex curve from C to E.

Any realistic retrieval system, being better than random but less than perfect, will lie between the lines for perfect retrieval and for random retrieval, starting at or near 100% precision, then decaying in a concave curve until it eventually reaches E. The better the performance, the closer the realistic curve will be to the perfect retrieval curve, as indicated by the arrow.

The Relationship between Precision and Recall

Since both recall and precision have been plotted against total retrieval, they can be plotted against each other, as shown in figure 13.

With random retrieval, precision tends to 10% regardless of recall and so is shown as the horizontal dotted line (DE).

A perfect retrieval system yields only relevant items until no more are left, so precision starts at 100% at F and continues horizontally at 100% across the top of the graph from F to A until recall is complete. After that point, when only nonrelevant items remain to be retrieved, recall is unaffected but precision is reduced, so the line falls vertically from A to E.

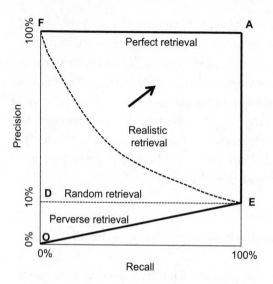

Figure 13 The relationship between precision and recall for random, perfect, perverse, and realistic retrieval.

With perverse retrieval, the 900 nonrelevant items have to be retrieved before the first relevant item. During the retrieval of those first 900, both precision and recall are at zero, so the line remains at the origin (O). When, finally, only relevant items remain to be retrieved, both precision and recall begin to rise in an almost flat concave curve from O to E.

The curve for realistic retrieval, as before, lies between the lines for random and perfect retrieval. The line should start at or near 100% precision (near F) and then form a downward, concave curve, eventually reaching E when the entire collection has been retrieved. In this, as in the other graphs, the more effective the retrieval system, the nearer the curve will be to the perfect curve, as indicated by the arrow.

The advantage of drawing curves for both perfect and perverse retrieval is that they define the space of possible retrieval performance. The area between perfect retrieval and random retrieval defines the realistic region of practical retrieval systems. Within this region all retrieval performances that are better than random necessarily have downward sloping curves in figure 13. In other words, a trade-off between precision and recall is unavoidable for any retrieval system that performs better than randomly.

The traditional criterion in the evaluation of selection systems is relevance, the most central concept in the field. The idea is that all and only relevant items should be selected, but this simple wish is deeply problematic in multiple ways. "Relevant" could be those items wanted or needed by the inquirer, those that will please or be most useful. However, want, need, please and useful are not the same, and assessments will be highly subjective—and, since the search is presumed to be by someone inadequately informed, likely to be unreliable. Relevance is highly situational, depending on what the inquirer already knows, and unstable, because the inquirer is, or should be, actively learning. The standard assumption that all items are independent, in the sense that the relevance of one item does not affect the relevance of any other item, is a convenient but unconvincing simplification. If two documents are very similar, one usually does not need both. Further, the goals of *all* relevant items and *only* relevant items are in conflict, because in practice one can seek to emphasize *all* (recall) only at the expense of *only* (precision), or vice versa.

Summary

In hindsight, it can be seen that the inverse relationship found is entailed by the way retrieval effectiveness is formulated: if all items are characterized as either relevant or nonrelevant, then any initial success in picking out relevant items necessarily has the effect of impoverishing the pool of items remaining to be retrieved, so retrieval performance must progressively deteriorate. Although the notion of relevance is easy to understand, it resists being operationalized in practice, and we must fall back on crude but practical substitutions.

FURTHER READING

There are large literatures available on most of the topics in this small book. Reference can also be made to relevant textbooks, including Bawden and Robinson (2013), Davis and Shaw (2011), Feather (2013), Glushko (2013), Norton (2010), and Rubin (2010). For sociological aspects, see Webster (2014), and for relevant technology see Gleick (2011). More generally, good starting points are the *Encyclopedia of Library and Information Sciences* (2010) and *LISA Library and Information Science Abstracts* (1969).

Parts of the text are adapted from earlier publications, where additional sources are noted that can supplement the few references in this text.

Chapter 1, "Introduction," draws on Buckland (2015b). See Furner (2004) for alternatives to the word information. The passport discussion is from Buckland (2014). See Day (2001) for the popularity of "information." Floridi (2010) provides a concise introduction to formal theories of information: entropy, Shannon-Weaver information theory, and more. For philology and the study of texts, see McGann (2014). The division of labor and secondhand knowledge is based on Wilson (1983). Day (2014) examines how information systems increasingly shape our lives.

Chapter 2, "Document and Evidence," is based on Buckland (2015b). The discussion of documents draws on Buckland (1991 and 1997) and Lund (2009), and the discussion of data management on Buckland (2011). On the history of copying, see Buckland (2012a). For Schrettinger, see Garrett (1999); for Otlet, see Wright (2014); for Ostwald, see Hapke (1999); and for Fleck, see Fleck (1979) and Cohen and Schnelle (1986). Blum (1980) and McKenzie (1999) are good sources for bibliography.

In chapter 3, "Individual and Community," Tylor's definition of culture is from Tylor (1871, 1). The complexity and difficulties of examining information-related behavior has made progress difficult. Case (2012) provides a good introduction. Earlier discussions include Wilson (1981) and Pettigrew, Fidel, and Bruce (2001). Discussion of "small worlds" draws on the work of Elfreda Chatman (e.g., Chatman 1992). For the social role of documents, see Brown and Duguid (2000) and Ferraris (2013). For a convenient introduction to the construction of knowledge, see Zerubavel (1997) as well as Mannheim (1936, chap. 1) and Berger and Luckmann (1966). See McGann (1983) and McKenzie (1999) for the social context of books.

Chapter 4, "Organizing: Arrangement and Description," draws on Buckland (1989; 2007) as well as Fairthorne (1961, 84–85).

Chapter 5, "Naming," is based on Buckland (2007 and 2012b) and also draws on Ranganathan (1951, 34), Suominen (1997), Briet (1954, 43; 2006, 50–51),

Fairthorne (1961), Blair (1990), Lakoff (1987), Frohmann (2004), Bowker and Star (2000), and Berman (1971).

Chapter 6, "Metadata," is based on Buckland (2006 and 2015a). For ideas and documentation as infrastructure, also see Foucault (1970) and Day (2007 and 2014). For space and place, see Buckland et al. (2007). For events and time, see Petras, Larson, and Buckland (2006). For biographical records see the Text Encoding Initiative Consortium (2009) and Buckland and Ramos (2010).

Chapter 7, "Discovery and Selection," is based on Buckland and Plaunt (1994), which was extensively developed in Plaunt (1997). For a printed bibliography as an interface, see Bates (1976). The semantic/syntactic theme is developed in Warner (2010).

Chapter 8, "Evaluation of Selection Methods," summarizes parts of Buckland and Gey (1994), which are presented in more detail in Appendix B. White (2010) provides an excellent discussion of relevance theory.

In Chapter 9, "Summary and Reflections," the section "What kind of field?" is based on Buckland (2012c). Bawden (2001) and Chevillotte (2010) provide useful reviews of the literature on information literacy.

Appendix A, "Anatomy of Selection," summarizes parts of Buckland and Plaunt (1994). Plaunt (1997) provides a more thorough treatment.

Appendix B, "Retrieval Evaluation," is based on Buckland and Gey (1994). Egghe (2008) provides a mathematic treatment of these relationships.

GLOSSARY

Authority list
In order to reduce ambiguities and inconsistencies in indexing terms, *vocabulary control* is exercised by making and using only *preferred terms* from an *authority list* with cross-references from nonpreferred terms to *preferred terms*.

Bibliography
1. Study or description of books and other publications. 2. A list of books or other publications.

Culture
Commonly used for "high culture," such as opera, classical music, and art exhibitions, *culture* is used in this book in its academic sense: how we live our daily lives. In a commonly cited definition, "culture or civilization, taken in its wide ethnographic sense, is that complex whole which includes knowledge, belief, art, morals, law, custom and any other capabilities and habits acquired by man as a member of society" (Tylor 1871, 1).

Document
Record, usually a text; more generally, something regarded by someone as evidence of something.

Epistemology
The study of knowledge itself.

Facet
A distinct aspect resulting from a basic division; for example, what, when, where, who, why, and how are distinct and different facets of an event.

Filtering
Selecting from a flow of records by matching them against a stable query.

Hypertext
Text with passages that are linked to other passages.

Infrastructure
Ancillary resources that enable an undertaking to function. Originally used to refer to structures used for transportation and military operations, *infrastructure* has been gradually extended to include services ancillary to, or in support of, the performance of any large-scale undertaking.

Intersubjective
Subjective states shared by two or more individuals.

Metadata
Literally, beyond or with data. A common name for descriptions of documents, records, and data; data about data.

Phenomenology
The study of experience and consciousness.

Phenomenon
Something perceived.

Photolithography
Printing using printing plates with images created photographically.

Photostat
A photographic image made with a camera directly onto paper without an intermediate negative. An important document copying technique in the early twentieth century.

Postcoordinate search
In information retrieval, when two or more concepts can be combined in a search query at the time of search. *See also* precoordinate indexing.

Precision
The proportion of documents that are relevant within a retrieved set in information retrieval.

Precoordinate indexing
Indexing systems in which combinations of concepts are created as needed at the time of indexing. *See also* postcoordinate search.

Preferred terms
When indexing, *vocabulary control* is maintained by using only *preferred terms* on an *authority list*, with cross references from nonpreferred terms to preferred terms.

Prosopography
Study of a set of persons.

Provenance
The chronology of the ownership, custody, or location of a document or historical object.

Recall
In information retrieval, the proportion of all relevant items in a collection that have been retrieved by a search.

Relevance
In information retrieval, the criterion of being a suitable response to a query.

Relevant
In information retrieval, considered to be a suitable response to a query.

Retrieval
A general term used for finding procedures, such as identifying (discovering the existence of documents); locating ("look-up," when identified objects have known addresses); fetching (bringing an object from a known address); and selecting (in the sense of choosing).

Semiotics
The theory and study of signs and symbols, especially the meanings of words and documents.

Vocabulary control
Limitation of index terms to *preferred terms*, with cross-references from nonpreferred terms to preferred terms.

REFERENCES

Bawden, David. 2001. Information and digital literacies: A review of concepts. *Journal of Documentation* 57 (2): 218–259.

Bawden, David, and Lyn Robinson. 2013. *Introduction to information science*. Chicago: Neal-Schuman.

Berger, Peter L., and Thomas Luckmann. 1966. *The social construction of reality: A treatise in the sociology of knowledge*. Garden City, NY: Doubleday.

Berman, Sanford. 1971. *Prejudices and antipathies: A tract on the LC subject heads concerning people*. Metuchen, NJ: Scarecrow.

Blair, David C. 1990. *Language and representation in information retrieval*. Amsterdam: Elsevier Science.

Blum, Rudolf. 1980. *Bibliographia: An inquiry into its definition and designations*. Chicago: American Library Association.

Bowker, Geoffrey, and Susan Leigh Star. 1999. *Sorting things out: Classification and its consequences*. Cambridge, MA: MIT Press.

Briet, Suzanne. 1951. *Qu'est-ce que la documentation?* Paris: EDIT.

Briet, Suzanne. 1954. Bibliothécaires et documentalistes. *Revue de la Documentation* 21, fasc. 2: 41-45.

Briet, Suzanne. 2006. *What is documentation?*, ed. Ronald E. Day. Lanham, MD: Scarecrow. Translation of S. Briet. 1951. *Qu'est-ce que la documentation?* Paris: EDIT.

Brown, John S., and Paul Duguid. 2000. *The social life of information*. Boston: Harvard Business School Press.

Buckland, Michael K. 1989. The roles of collections and the scope of collection development. *Journal of Documentation* 45 (3): 213–226.

Buckland, Michael K. 1991. Information as thing. *Journal of the American Society for Information Science* 42 (5): 351–360. http://people.ischool.berkeley.edu/~buckland/thing.html.

Buckland, Michael K. 1997. What is a "document"? *Journal of the American Society for Information Science* 48 (9): 804–809. http://people.ischool.berkeley .edu/~buckland/whatdoc.html.

Buckland, Michael K. 2006. Description and search: Metadata as infrastructure. *Brazilian Journal of Information Science* 0 (0): 3–14. http://www2.marilia .unesp.br/revistas/index.php/bjis/article/view/26/47.

Buckland, Michael K. 2007. Naming in the library: Marks, meaning and machines. In *Nominalization, nomination and naming in texts*, eds. Christian Todenhagen and Wolfgang Thiele, 249–260. Tübingen: Stauffenburg. http:// people.ischool.berkeley.edu/~buckland/naminglib.pdf.

Buckland, Michael K. 2011. Data management as bibliography. *Bulletin of the American Society for Information Science and Technology* 37 (6): 34–37. http://asis.org/Bulletin/Aug-11/AugSep11_Buckland.pdf.

Buckland, Michael K. 2012a. Lodewyk Bendikson and photographic techniques in documentation, 1910–1943. In *International perspectives on the history of information science and technology*, eds. Toni Carbo and Trudi B. Hahn, 99–106. Medford, NJ: Information Today.

Buckland, Michael K. 2012b. Obsolescence in subject description. *Journal of Documentation* 68(2):154–161. http://people.ischool.berkeley.edu/~buckland/ obsolsubject.pdf.

Buckland, Michael K. 2012c. What kind of a science can information science be? *Journal of the American Society for Information Science and Technology* 63 (1): 1–7. http://people.ischool.berkeley.edu/~buckland/whatsci.pdf.

Buckland, Michael K. 2014. Documentality beyond documents. *Monist* 97 (2): 179–186. http://people.ischool.berkeley.edu/~buckland/docbeyonddoc.pdf.

Buckland, Michael K. 2015a. Classification, links and contexts. In *Classification and authority control: Expanding resources discovery*, eds. Aida Slavic and M. I. Cordeiro, 1–16. Proceedings of the International UDC Seminar, October 29–30 2015, Lisbon, Portugal. Würzburg: Ergon Verlag. Revised text at http:// people.ischool.berkeley.edu/~buckland/lisbon15.pdf.

Buckland, Michael K. 2015b. Document theory: An introduction. In *Records, archives and memory: Selected papers from the Conference and School on Records, Archives and Memory Studies*, eds. Mirna Willer, Anne J. Gilliland, and Marijana

Tomić, 223–237. Zadar: University of Zadar Press. http://people.ischool.berkeley
.edu/~buckland/zadardoctheory.pdf.

Buckland, Michael K., Aitao Chen, Fredric C. Gey, Ray R. Larson, Ruth Mostern,
and Vivien Petras. 2007. Geographic search: Catalogs, gazetteers, and maps.
College and Research Libraries 68 (5): 376–387. http://crl.acrl.org/content/
68/5/376.full.pdf+html.

Buckland, Michael K., and Fredric Gey. 1994. The relationship between recall
and precision. *Journal of the American Society for Information Science* 45 (1):
12–19.

Buckland, Michael K., and Christian Plaunt. 1994. On the construction of
selection systems. *Library Hi Tech* 48: 15–28. http://people.ischool.berkeley
.edu/~buckland/papers/analysis/analysis.html.

Buckland, Michael K., and Michele R. Ramos. 2010. Events as a structuring
device in biographical mark-up and metadata. *Bulletin of the American Society
for Information Science and Technology* 36 (2): 26–29. http://www.asis.org/
Bulletin/Dec-09/Bulletin_DecJan10_Final.pdf.

Case, Donald O. 2012. *Looking for information: A survey of research on information
seeking, needs and behavior*. 3rd ed. Bingley, UK: Emerald Group.

Chatman, Elfreda A. 1992. *The information world of retired women*. New York:
Greenwood Press.

Chevillotte, Sylvie. 2010. Information literacy. In *Encyclopedia of library and
information sciences*, ed. Marcia J. Bates, 2421–2428. 3rd ed. Boca Raton, FL:
CRC Press.

Cohen, Robert S., and Thomas Schnelle, eds. 1986. *Cognition and fact: Materials
on Ludwik Fleck*. Boston Studies in the Philosophy of Science, 87. Dordrecht:
Reidel.

Davis, Charles H., and Debora Shaw, eds. 2011. *Introduction to information science and technology*. Medford, NJ: Information Today.

Day, Ronald E. 2001. *The modern invention of information: Discourse, history, and
power*. Carbondale: Southern Illinois University Press.

Day, Ronald E. 2007. "A necessity of our time": Suzanne Briet's "*What is
documentation?*" In *A document (re)turn: Contributions from a research field in*

transition, eds. Roswitha Skare, Niels W. Lund, and Andreas Vårheim, 312–326. Frankfurt am Main: Peter Lang.

Day, Ronald E. 2014. *Indexing it all: The subject in the age of documentation, information, and data*. Cambridge, MA: MIT Press.

Dewey, Melvil. 1899. *Decimal classification and relativ index for libraries, clippings, notes, etc*. 6th ed. Boston: Library Bureau.

Egghe, Leo. 2008. The measures precision, recall, fallout, and miss as a function of the number of retrieved documents and their mutual interrelations. *Information Processing and Management* 44: 856–876.

Encyclopedia of library and information sciences, ed. Marcia J. Bates. 2010. 3rd ed. 7 vols. Boca Raton, FL: CRC Press. http://www.tandfonline.com/doi/book/10.1081/E-ELIS3.

Fairthorne, Robert A. 1961. *Towards information retrieval*. London: Butterworths.

Feather, John. 2013. *The information society: A study of continuity and change*. London: Facet.

Ferraris, Maurizio. 2013. *Documentality: Why it is necessary to leave traces*. New York: Fordham University Press.

Fleck, Ludwik. 1979. *Genesis and development of a scientific fact*, trans. Frederick Bradley and Thaddeus J. Trenn. Chicago: University of Chicago Press. Translation of *Entwicklung einer wissenschaftlichen Tatsache*. Basel: Schwabe, 1935.

Floridi, Luciano. 2010. *Information: A very short introduction*. Oxford University Press.

Foucault, Michel. 1970. *The order of things: An archaeology of the human sciences*. New York: Vintage Books.

Frohmann, Bernd. 2004. *Deflating information: From science studies to documentation*. Toronto: University of Toronto Press.

Furner, Jonathan. 2004. Information studies without information. *Library Trends* 52 (3): 427–446.

Garrett, Jeffrey. 1999. Redefining order in the German library, 1755–1825. *Eighteenth-Century Studies* 33: 103–123.

Gleick, James. 2011. *The information: A history, a theory, a flood*. New York: Pantheon Books.

Glushko, Robert J., ed. 2013. *The discipline of organizing*. Cambridge, MA: MIT Press.

Hapke, Thomas. 1999. Wilhelm Ostwald, the "Brücke" (Bridge), and connections to other bibliographic activities at the beginning of the twentieth century. In *Proceedings of the 1998 Conference on the History and Heritage of Science Information Systems*, eds. Mary Ellen Bowden, Trudi Bellardo Hahn, and Robert V. Williams, 139–147. Medford, NJ: Information Today. http://wayback.archive-it.org/2118/20101023161313/http://assets.chemheritage.org/explore/ASIS_documents/ASIS98_Hapke.pdf.

Lakoff, George. 1987. *Women, fire, and dangerous things: What categories reveal about the mind*. Chicago: University of Chicago Press.

LISA Library and Information Science Abstracts. 1969- . [Electronic Resource]. Ann Arbor, MI: ProQuest. http://www.proquest.com/products-services/lisa-set-c.html.

Lund, Niels W. 2009. Document theory. *Annual Review of Information Science and Technology* 43: 399–432.

Mannheim, Karl. 1936. *Ideology and utopia: An introduction to the sociology of knowledge*. New York: Harcourt, Brace.

McGann, Jerome. 1983. *A critique of modern textual criticism*. Chicago: University of Chicago Press.

McGann, Jerome. 2014. *A new republic of letters: Memory and scholarship in the age of digital reproduction*, 19. Cambridge, MA: Harvard University Press.

McKenzie, Donald F. 1999. *Bibliography and the sociology of texts*. Cambridge, UK: Cambridge University Press.

Norton, Melanie J. 2010. *Introductory concepts in information science*. 2nd ed. Medford, NJ: Information Today.

Pettigrew, Karen E., Raya Fidel, and Harry Bruce. 2001. Conceptual frameworks in information behavior. *Annual Review of Information Science and Technology* 35: 43–78.

Petras, Vivien. 2006. Translating dialects in search: Mapping between specialized languages of discourse and documentary languages. Ph. D. thesis.

University of California, Berkeley. http://www.sims.berkeley.edu/~vivienp/diss/vpetras-dissertation2006-official.pdf.

Petras, Vivien, Ray R. Larson, and Michael K. Buckland. 2006. Time period directories: A metadata infrastructure for placing events in temporal and geographic context. In *Opening information horizons*, 151–160. Proceedings of the 6th ACM/IEEE-CS Joint Conference on Digital Libraries. New York: Association for Computing Machinery. http://portal.acm.org/citation.cfm?id=1141782.

Plaunt, Christian J. 1997. A functional model of information retrieval systems. Ph. D. thesis. University of California, Berkeley.

Ranganathan, Shiyali Ramamrita. 1951. *Classification and communication*. Delhi: University of Delhi.

Rubin, Richard E. 2010. *Foundations of library and information science*. 3rd ed. New York: Neal-Schuman.

Suominen, Vesa. 1997. *Filling empty space: A treatise on semiotic structures in information retrieval, in documentation, and in related research*. Acta Universitatis Ouluensis, Series B, Humaniora, 27. Oulu, Finland: Oulu University Press.

Text Encoding Initiative Consortium. 2009. Report on XML mark-up of biographical and prosopographical data. http://www.tei-c.org/Activities/Workgroups/PERS/persw02.xml.

Tylor, Edward B. 1871. *Primitive culture*. London: Murray.

Warner, Julian. 2010. *Human information retrieval*. Cambridge, MA: MIT Press.

Webster, Frank. 2014. *Theories of the information society*. 4th ed. London: Routledge.

White, Howard D. 2010. Relevance in theory. In *Encyclopedia of library and information sciences*, ed. Marcia J. Bates. Vol. 6, 4498–4511. 3rd ed. Boca Raton, FL: CRC Press.

Wilson, Patrick. 1968. *Two kinds of power: An essay on bibliographical control*. Berkeley: University of California Press. http://www.ucpress.edu/op.php?isbn=9780520035157.

Wilson, Patrick. 1983. *Second-hand knowledge: An inquiry into cognitive authority*. Westport, CT: Greenwood.

Wilson, T. D. 1981. On user studies and information needs. *Journal of Documentation* 37 (1): 3–15.

Wright, Alex. 2014. *Cataloging the world: Paul Otlet and the birth of the information age*. Oxford University Press.

Zerubavel, Eviatar. 1997. *Social mindscapes: An invitation to cognitive sociology*. Cambridge, MA: Harvard University Press.

INDEX

MICHAEL BUCKLAND is Emeritus Professor in the School of Information at the University of California, Berkeley, and Codirector of the Electronic Cultural Atlas Initiative there.